1

Book Cover image
Bigstock.com/Holbox

ISBN-13: 978-1484089248

EMIGRATING TO FLORIDA

The Complete Brit's Guide

Disclaimer

Every effort has been made to ensure that Emigrating to Florida, the Complete Brit's Guide is as accurate as possible. However, typographical and/or content errors may exist and this book should only be used for information and entertainment purposes. The book is sold with the understanding that neither the author nor the publisher are rendering any legal, tax or financial or other professional advice or services and is based solely upon the author's personal and professional experience and research and is believed to be accurate at the time of publication. Questions regarding legal, tax, financial and copyright law should be addressed to competent members of those professional areas. The author and publisher shall have neither liability nor responsibility to any person or entity with respect to any loss or damage caused, or alleged to be caused, directly or indirectly by the information contained in this book.

Contents

Introduction

So why would anyone consider leaving England? It is after all a country steeped in history and tradition; quaint villages, rolling countryside, seasons, fish and chips, a free health service, unarmed police, the royal family – well maybe not the royal family, but I can't deny that Britain does have some great things going for it.

On the other hand, the thought of trading rain, freezing temperatures and grey overcast skies for clear blue ones and a sub-tropical climate comes unsurprisingly as a major appeal to many. Throw in some common British concerns such as anti-social behavior, housing costs, rises in immigration and strains on public services and together with some spirit of adventure, you have all the right ingredients to let go of your day job and pick up your passport.

My spouse had been talking about emigrating for a couple of years but I hadn't seriously considered it until we started a family. Having children led me to look more carefully at the environment I would be raising them in and wonder what Britain would be evolving into in the years to come. Emigrating is a hard decision to make. You are leaving behind family, friends, a job, home, familiar surroundings and a familiar way of life. Our journey has been expensive, stressful and caused much heartache to our relatives, but overall I have loved our experience thus far, and if I had to return to Britain, it would be kicking and screaming.

I have lived in Florida for 6 years now. I enjoy leaving the house wearing shorts and flip flops and into a warm, blue skied environment. I'm fortunate to own a large home, complete with swimming pool and lake views for the same price as my small house back in England close to railway tracks and on an overcrowded estate. I admire the patriotism and pride that Americans have in their country, their community spirit, and despite the perception of a violent America and complete with gun crime, I actually feel safer and less intimidated going out than I did in Britain.

Florida of course is by no means Utopia. Some of its downsides I knew before making the move, while others I discovered within my first couple of years of living there. This book serves to provide an insight into the realities of living in Florida from a British perspective. Arriving in the Sunshine State, my knowledge was also limited on fundamental aspects of Florida such as the education system, the weather or just how dangerous that insect was that just landed on my child. If only there had been some type of British guide about moving to the area that would have assisted me with making the transition. Well for all those others taking the plunge, here is that guide.

Chapter 1

Making the Move

So you have decided to leave Britain. What was it that tipped you over the edge? A little tired of the cold, damp rainy weather? Fed up walking past abusive youths in hoodies? Maybe you've had one too many bad experiences from a British public service or just feel like half of Europe has moved into the country.

The reason you want to leave is because you suspect that it's better elsewhere. You've seen pictures of Australian beaches, felt the warmth of Florida sunshine on that Disney trip last year, or maybe know someone that emigrated to Canada and despite those cold winters you hear they're loving every minute of it.

After careful consideration you have decided that Florida is the destination for you. Good choice. English speaking, similar culture and a lot less cold than Canada. Okay, it does have some gun issues, scary wildlife and a few hurricanes now and then but we'll get to that later.

Are you ready to leave behind family and friends? Make irreversible decisions such as quitting your job or selling your home? Are you willing to gamble your current lifestyle and financial situation for the possibility of something better for you and your family?

Well with any luck, you're not that fond of your job anyway and your family is promising to visit you regularly once you settle in. I'm sure it's because they are really close to you and has nothing to do with the fact that your new home will be within driving distance of Orlando, theme park capital of the world!

Emigrating is a huge undertaking. You are leaving behind your current and familiar way of life and starting again in an unknown and foreign land, usually without family and friends around you for support. That takes some bravery. This is a mammoth challenge ahead of you and one that will test you physically, mentally and emotionally.

Research

The more research, planning and preparation you can do, the smoother your transition will be. Speak to as many people as you can who have made the move themselves. Expat forums such as 'Brits in America', 'British Expats' and 'Expat Forum' are all excellent sources for this. These sites provide you with the opportunity to communicate with Brits that have moved to many different countries and many are more than happy to share their experiences, answer questions and provide you with advice.

Immigration

As much as you may want to live in the U.S, you will first need an approved immigration method in order to reside there. Further details are provided in Chapter 13 but ways to enter for the British are typically via family, employment or through investment. Some routes provide permanent residency; others will only allow you and your family to live in the States on a temporary basis and with restrictions. Swallow the high hourly rate fee and make sure you have visited an immigration lawyer to discuss the best entry method available to you.

The Expense

Unfortunately emigrating can often be an expensive process. You may have already planned for such things as; immigration fees, flights, accommodation, furniture and vehicles at your new destination, but there will inevitably be a myriad of other expenses along the way that is bound to come as an unwelcome surprise to you. As an example, deposits will be required for many necessary things that you will be attempting to purchase on arrival, such as utilities for your home and mobile phones for your family. Your spouse may also be raring to find employment (or not!) but may have to wait several months to receive their Employment Authorization Card from the U.S Citizen and Immigration Services allowing them to work. With these things in mind, the more funds you can scrape together for your venture the better.

Shipping

Now unless you are a ruthless neat freak, you are bound to have accumulated several possessions over the years. You may want to use a shipping company to transport these belongings or alternatively just cram as much as you can into your luggage allowance and sell or discard the rest. Although shipping your belongings is additional expense, it's worth considering as it can save you the cost of having to buy many replacement items at your new destination. You and your family may also be feeling a little homesick six weeks into your new life and receiving a crate filled with familiar items from back home can be a great way to boost your family's spirits.

Property Issues

If you own your home, you will also need to decide what to do with it. Selling might provide you with much needed equity for your new venture and eliminate a major financial obligation. What happens though if you end up returning to the U.K in the future? Would you like that home to go back to? Would you be able to purchase or rent a new British home with limited funds for a deposit and perhaps no employment for a while?

Alternatively, do you think you would be safer renting out your property for now with the benefit of having a tenant repaying that mortgage for you? Will you have the time and inclination to deal with tenancy issues when you are throwing yourself into your new life? When the British property is vacant, will you be able to pay the mortgage and council tax using your hard earned U.S wages that don't convert so handsomely back to British pounds?

Taking Your Pet

Taking pets with you requires some further tasks. You will need to make arrangements with both your local vet and the airline that you're flying with. There is no quarantine for pets arriving in Florida but they are subject to inspection at ports of entry for evidence of infectious diseases that can be transmitted to humans. You will also need your vet to issue an International Health Certificate within ten days of departure to certify that your pet is in good health to fly.

The airlines have strict guidelines on transporting your pet and you will need to obtain a travel cage that meets specific requirements. Although it's not necessary to have one in order to enter the U.S, it's worth obtaining a Pet Passport before travel. By doing so, your pet will be able to re-enter the U.K with ease and without quarantine in the event of you returning to Britain. To receive a Pet Passport, animals must be micro chipped, vaccinated, given a blood test and tapeworm treatment. More details can be obtained from your vet.

Leaving Family & Friends

Although you may be excited at starting your new life, saying goodbye to family and friends can be heart wrenching. If you are planning on keeping in contact with your loved ones through regular transatlantic visits so much the better but financial, health, work commitments and other factors can in reality often prevent this. Fortunately, modern technology provides a variety of ways for us to communicate with loved ones back home. Skype, webcams, Facebook and cheap international calling are all excellent ways to bridge that gap between visits.

Having made all your preparations, you are ready to take that plunge. You are tired of what Britain has to offer and are eager to start a new and better life for you and your family. Filled with both excitement and trepidation, you head off to the airport. Laden with tickets, passports and a stackful of suitcases you make that daring leap into what is sure to be one of your biggest adventures yet.

Chapter 2

Arrival in the Sunshine State

Its 28°C, with blue skies overhead and not a grey cloud as far as the eye can see. Dressed in shorts and flip flops you are surrounded by temptation. Swimming pools, theme parks, restaurants, shopping malls and white sandy beaches all beckon you. Maybe you'll give yourself a bit of time to enjoy some of these pleasures - it is after all, one of the reasons you moved here. Remember though that this isn't a holiday. Florida is your home now and you have an important 'To-Do' list that requires your urgent attention.

Accommodation

If you flew out to Florida on an earlier mission and secured accommodation ready for your arrival then full brownie points to you. If however, you're staying with friends, family or living out of a hotel room for now, then finding a place to live is going to be your No.1 priority.

Whether you rent or buy will be a big decision for you. You may well want to test the waters of Florida living before purchasing a property and unless you have a large deposit to put down, your lack of U.S credit history will make it more difficult to obtain a mortgage or at least one with a decent percentage rate.

Should you decide on the rental approach, properties in Florida are typically leased out on a seven or twelve month basis and most will require a deposit of at least one month's rent in advance, a credit history check and a couple of decent references. You will usually be responsible for all utility bills and lawn care services associated with the home but unlike Britain, property tax

25

(council tax) remains the responsibility of the property owner.

Opening a Bank Account

You will need to visit a bank in person in order to open an account. There is a variety to choose from, but it may be more worthwhile going to a major national bank rather than a local one where they are likely to be more familiar with dealing with foreign nationals. The Internal Revenue Service requires all financial institutions to ascertain the applicant's tax identification number so you will need to produce either your social security number or if you don't have one, your individual identification taxpayer number (ITIN) instead. Further information on ITINs and how to obtain one can be found on page 28. Additionally, you will need to bring your passport and any other means of primary identification such as drivers licence and proof of current residency. You will also need to make a deposit so don't forget to bring some cash!

Obtaining your Florida Driver's License

After arriving in Florida, residents have thirty days in which to obtain their Florida driver's license and to get your hands on one, you will need to take a driving test. For those who still have vivid memories of undertaking a grueling 45 minute driving exam around town, complete with parallel parking, fear not. The State's driving exam consists of a theory test of 40 'Highway Code' type questions, an eye-sight and hearing test, and successful completion of certain vehicle manoeuvres which I performed in the company of my examiner around the Department's car park. It's not at all difficult to do and goes some way to explain the standard of driving on Florida roads.

Your drivers' licence acts in many ways like a State I.D card. You will be asked for it whenever you need to produce identification, address verification and more often than not, whenever you attempt to buy alcohol. How often you need to renew it depends on the status in which you are living in the U.S. E2 visa holders for example, are only provided with a temporary driver's licence which needs renewal every 12 months. Permanent residents (green card holders) can receive a licence valid for 8 years.

Social Security Numbers

A social security number (SSN) is similar in principle to our National Insurance number. It's needed for employment, for tax purposes and to draw social security later in life. All U.S citizens and permanent residents are entitled to receive one, as are temporary residents once they are authorized to work in the U.S.

Many Americans are now allocated their social security number at birth. For all others, details on how to obtain one can be found at the Social Security Administration's website at: www.ssa.gov.

Social security numbers are much more widely used than our National Insurance numbers, so much so, that the majority of Americans will know their nine digit number off by heart. This is largely because their SSN's are regularly requested from them by many institutes and companies who routinely use them to identify and verify their clients. This is particularly true in the finance industry where social security numbers are typically required in order to open a bank account or apply for a loan or other line of credit.

The Social Security Administration operates a strict policy and will not provide someone with a social security number unless they meet the criteria. This can be problematic for non-permanent residents who will only be given a number if they are authorized to work in the U.S. Those ineligible are often stay at home mums and their children living in the States on temporary visas. You will find that without an SSN, obtaining services from some companies can prove very difficult, even to the extent of trying to obtain a mobile phone. With this in mind, if you are eligible for an SSN, you can save yourself some headaches by applying for one at your earliest opportunity.

Social security numbers are also required for tax purposes. For those ineligible for a number, the IRS kindly issues them instead with an Individual Taxpayer Identification number (ITIN) so that they can still pay their taxes. Children can also be given an ITIN so that parents can claim tax credits for their dependants on their annual tax returns. More details and ways to apply for a tax identification number can be found on the Internal Revenue Services' website at www.irs.gov.

Employment Authorization Cards

Permanent residents (green card holders) have the right to both live and work in the United States. However for many living in America on temporary visas approval to work must first be obtained through the United States Citizen and Immigration Services (USCIS).

Permission comes in the form of receiving an 'Employment Authorization Card' sometimes known as a 'work permit'. You can apply for one either by going through the services of an immigration lawyer or by doing it yourself if you're feeling confident. The application form (Form I-765) can be found on their website at www.uscis.gov, and if you are doing it yourself, you will need to make sure that you submit all supporting documentation with the application form such as copies of your passport, visa, I-94 arrival/departure card etc. The cost to submit the form is currently $380. Using the services of a lawyer will cost you extra.

Unfortunately, the main problem with needing an Employment Authorization Card is the time it takes to obtain one. Wait times are typically between three and four months and you will be unable to commence any employment in the meantime. Additionally, the cards usually only have a lifespan of between 15 -24 months before needing renewal. Here lies the problem. The earliest you can apply to renew your card is four months before its expiry but it can also take over four months to receive a new one! Many find their jobs endangered because if they don't receive the new cards in time, they can no longer legally work and face termination from their employer.

If you only have a few weeks left before expiry and have not yet received a new card, it is worthwhile contacting the USCIS in an attempt to expedite your application. Their website advises that if you have not received your card within 90 days of applying, an interim one can be issued in the meantime, but when I visited my local immigration office to obtain one as instructed by the website, I was informed that they had never heard of such a thing and I came away empty handed. One last thing to note is that every time you apply for a new card, you will need another $380.

Obtaining a Vehicle

In Britain, you can often get away with either walking or using public transport to reach your destination. This is not the case in the U.S and owning a vehicle is typically a necessity. Ideally, you will have brought enough funds with you to be able to purchase either a new or used vehicle outright. If however, you require a car loan, be prepared for a high interest rate due to your lack of U.S credit history.

You can choose either an automatic or manual but the majority of Americans drive automatics. Both new and used cars can be purchased from car dealerships but be warned, car salesmen are as unscrupulous as politicians and unless you have your wits about you, you are likely to be short-changed. The advertised price of a vehicle is not the price you have to pay and in many cases you can negotiate at least a few thousand dollars off the advertised price. The exception to this is car dealerships that advertise 'no haggle' policies such as 'Car Max'. (www.carmax.com). With this company, the price advertised is the price you pay and many people prefer this method than having to spend hours negotiating to get a decent price with a salesman.

Once purchased, the vehicle will need to be registered in your name. You can do so by visiting your local Department of Highway and Motor Vehicle office but it's often done for you by the dealership if you purchased the vehicle through them.

In Florida, license plates (number plates) on vehicles belong to the owner of the vehicle not the vehicle itself. Therefore, when it comes to selling your car, you will need to remove the plate and affix it to your new vehicle. When you first arrive in Florida you won't have a licence plate. The dealership can order one for you and will give you a temporary one in the meantime. Alternatively you can apply for one through the Department of Highway and Motor Vehicles.

There is no 'MOT' in the U.S although vehicles must remain roadworthy. There is however an annual fee similar to our road tax – a registration fee for the vehicle every year. Once purchased, you receive a yellow sticker showing the date of its expiry which affixes to your rear license plate. The date of expiry falls on the registered owner's birthday so although it may be easy to remember the renewal date, it's not a great gift to receive on your special day.

Obtaining insurance for your vehicle is not as easy as finding a quote online as it is in Britain. Each insurance company has agents working and dealing with their clients on their behalf. You will need to select an insurance company that you are interested in and then contact the agent local for your area to obtain a quote and arrange a policy for you. Some agents work for multiple companies and can provide you with several quotes. The terminology of vehicle insurance is very different than in the U.K so it's best to sit down with the agent and find out exactly what your insurance does and does not cover.

School Enrollment

As a resident of the State of Florida, children between the ages of 5 and 18 are entitled to free education at a Public school regardless of their nationality and temporary or permanent legal status. To find which school is allocated to your neighbourhood, visit your County's education website. Here it will advise your school zoning (catchment area) and list the documentation you will need to bring to the school in order to register your child such as birth certificate, passport and verification of address.

To register your child you will also need to provide two specific health records which are typically provided by your child's U.S doctor. Children from Kindergarten to 12th Grade, who are making their initial entry into a Florida school must present a record of a physical examination completed within the past 12 months. The second required form is the Florida Certification of Immunization (Form 680) which documents the immunizations required for entry to Florida Schools. Travelling from Britain your child will almost certainly already have many of the immunizations required. There are however one or two extra that are required by Florida's education system such as the chickenpox vaccine.

Health Insurance

Health care is not free in the United States. Services are very expensive and without health insurance you run the risk of receiving a hospital bill for tens of thousands of dollars. Health insurance is often provided by U.S employers (they usually provide a significant portion of the cost with the employee contributing the remaining amount). If however, you're not working or are self-employed, you can obtain quotes for health insurance from various providers. The more popular, well known ones are United Healthcare, Blue Cross Blue Shield and Aetna. Be aware that some of these companies will not provide cover unless you are a permanent resident or U.S Citizen. Health coverage is particularly expensive and the cost will vary depending on your medical history and the amount of deductible (excess amount) that you choose. More detailed information on healthcare is provided in Chapter 8.

Chapter 3

The Weather

Florida weather is probably one of the biggest attractions for anyone thinking of immigrating to the State. The thought of avoiding rain, freezing temperatures and replacing grey overcast skies for cloudless blue ones comes as a major appeal to most. I like nothing better than leaving my home, work, restaurant or store, donning my sunglasses and feeling the warmth of the sunshine on my skin as I go out into the open air. I don't know much about the science behind seasonal affective disorder but what I do know is this: clear blue skies and warm weather make me happy - grey skies and cold weather do not.

As nice as the tropical climate is though, it does come at a price. Here are some factors that you need to be aware of when it comes to Florida weather:

Thunderstorms & Lightning

Before I arrived in Florida I knew very little about what to do in the event of a thunderstorm. My knowledge consisted of being told once that in the event of lightning, it wasn't wise to seek shelter under a tree. Why is it important for a Floridian to know a little about thunderstorms? Because Florida is the lightning capital of the United States!

Over the last ten years, lightning has killed an average of 39 people each year across the U.S and Florida averages 6 deaths and 39 injuries a year. In the Sunshine State, short thunderstorms are a common occurrence most afternoons during the summer months. As well as disrupting your outdoor afternoon plans, they can also making driving conditions quite hazardous.

The Florida Disaster Organization offers
the following Lightning Safety Advice

1. Once you see lightning or hear thunder, you should immediately go inside a house, building, or other enclosed structure.

2. Once indoors, do not use any corded electrical devices, avoid using plumbing, and stay away from doors and windows. The electrical current from lightning can travel through wires, cables and pipes.

3. If you are caught outside when a thunderstorm approaches and cannot make indoors quickly, avoid open areas.

4. Avoid water (swimming pools, lakes and rivers), beaches and boats.

5. When you can't make it to an enclosed building, the next best option is to get into a vehicle with a hard-topped roof. The steel frame of a hard-topped vehicle provides increased protection if you are not touching metal. Although you may be injured if lightning strikes your car, you are much safer inside a vehicle than outside.

6. Lightning often strikes outside of heavy rain and may occur as far as 10 miles away from any rainfall.

7. In the event that a person is struck by lightning, medical care may be needed immediately to save the person's life. Lightning victims do not carry an electrical charge and are safe to touch and help. Call 911, give first aid and if possible, move the victim to a safer place as lightning can strike twice.

Hurricanes

Florida's proximity to warm waters and the tropics comes with a disadvantage – Hurricanes. Hurricanes are tropical storms with winds that have reached a constant speed of 74 miles per hour or more. They are categorized on a scale of between 1-5 depending on wind strength, and they hit Florida more than any other State.

Hurricanes originate in the ocean as a result of a tropical disturbance. They bring with them torrential rains, high winds and storm surges which can lead to major damage, flooding and loss of electrical power.

Istockphoto/choicegraphx

The Atlantic hurricane season officially begins on June 1st through to November 30th but the peak months are August and September. It is not uncommon for residents living in the direct path of a hurricane that is about to hit landfall to have to evacuate their homes and in coastal regions you will see many evacuation route signs around the area. However, once they reach land, hurricanes tend to lose their power very rapidly.

Before the season begins it is wise to stock up with some emergency supplies in the event of a hurricane coming your way. Although you will get a few days' notice that the storm is approaching, the last thing you need is to be trying to grab supplies at the last minute. Remember that you could be confined to your home for long hours and without power, so it's essential to keep items such as; a torch, batteries, emergency food, water and a non-electric can opener readily accessible.

Hurricane Watch

An announcement that hurricane conditions (sustained winds of 74 mph or higher) are *possible* within the specified area. Because hurricane preparedness activities become difficult once winds reach tropical storm force, the hurricane watch is issued 48 hours in advance of the anticipated onset of tropical-storm-force winds.

Hurricane Warning

An announcement that hurricane conditions (sustained winds of 74 mph or higher) are *expected* somewhere within the specified area. Because hurricane preparedness activities become difficult once winds reach tropical storm force, the hurricane warning is issued 36 hours in advance of the anticipated onset of tropical-storm-force winds.

Tornados

A tornado is a violent whirlwind that usually develops in association with a severe thunderstorm. A typical tornado looks like a spinning gray funnel shaped cloud below the base of a thunderstorm cloud. Their deadly force can leave a trail of destruction and be fatal to anyone in its path.

The U.S averages about 1200 tornadoes each year but only about 20 of those are 'killer' tornadoes, claiming a total of about 60 lives. Although Florida is prone to tornados, they are relatively weak in comparison to other States. Whenever there is a threat of a tornado, a tornado 'watch' or 'warning' message is broadcast on your local television or radio.

Tornado Watch:

Tornadoes are possible in your area. Remain alert for approaching storms.

Tornado Warning:

A tornado has been sighted or indicated by weather radar. If a tornado warning is issued for your area and the sky becomes threatening, move to your pre-designated place of safety.

Tornado safety advice if a Warning is issued:

1. In a home or building, move to a pre-designated shelter, such as a basement. If an underground shelter is not available, move to an interior room or hallway on the lowest floor.

2. Stay away from windows.

3. Get out of automobiles. Do not try to outrun a tornado in your car.

4. Mobile homes, even if tied down, offer little protection from tornadoes and should be abandoned.

Florida Tornado Statistics:

Average per year: 49

Average Tornado Deaths per year: 3

Average Tornado Injuries per year: 60

Deadliest Tornado: February 22, 1998, a tornado in Kissimmee killed 25 people.

Hot Summers

As pleasant as the temperatures are during the winter, the summer months can get uncomfortably hot and humid. Air-conditioning in homes, offices and vehicles provide welcome relief indoors but once outside, that heat can be a major annoyance. It's not particularly pleasant climbing into a vehicle that's been baking in the August sun all day. Neither is it fun to take your kids on a ten minute walk to the local playground only to find them pouring with sweat by the time their reach their destination.

According to the Florida Department of Health, more than 3000 people are seen in emergency rooms each year for heat related illnesses. Heat Exhaustion can develop after exposure to high temperatures and not drinking enough water. Those who are most vulnerable to heat exhaustion are the elderly, infants, small children, individuals with medical conditions and those working or exercising in a hot environment.

Climate Data for Orlando, Florida

°C	Jan	Feb	Mch	Apr	May	Jun
Average High	22.1	23.3	26.0	28.3	31.2	32.8
Average Low	9.9	10.7	13.3	15.5	18.8	21.8

°C	Jul	Aug	Sep	Oct	Nov	Dec
Average High	33.4	33.3	32.4	29.4	26.1	22.9
Average Low	22.6	22.8	22.2	18.6	14.8	11.4

Provided by Florida Climate Center

TIPS FOR PREVENTING HEAT RELATED ILLNESSES
PROVIDED BY THE FLORIDA DEPT OF HEALTH

• **Drink plenty of fluids** that do not contain alcohol or large amounts of sugar. Limit sodas because of the added sugar and caffeine. Sweat is 99 percent water, so when you exercise or play, you lose water. Don't wait until you are thirsty to drink fluids and always make sure your water is clean. Add slices of fruit to water or drink 100 percent juice if you do not like the taste of water.

• **Limit outside activity** to morning and evening hours. Be cautious and stay out of the sun when exercising between 10:00 a.m. and 4:00 p.m. Children, seniors and persons with health problems should stay in the coolest available place, not necessarily indoors.

• **Rest often** in shady areas, or remain inside in an air conditioned space.

• **Dress for summer** by wearing lightweight, light-colored and loose fitting clothing to reflect heat and sun. Wear wide-brimmed hats to shade the sun.

• **Protect your eyes and skin** by wearing sunglasses and sunscreen. Use sunscreens with SPF 15 or higher that protect against both UVA and UVB rays. Sunburn reduces your body's ability to dissipate heat. Sunscreen should be applied every 2 to 4 hours, liberally enough to all sun-exposed areas that it forms a film when initially applied.

• **Do not leave children or pets in an unattended vehicle** because the temperature can reach 135 degrees in less than ten minutes.

Chapter 4

Living with Florida Wildlife

Although Britain does contain the odd species of dangerous wildlife, the only creatures I ever came face to face with in England were snails, frogs and the occasional harmless house spider. Florida on the other hand is an entirely different matter! This chapter focuses on some of the critters you are likely to encounter living in the State including some of the more dangerous wildlife to be aware of.

Alligators

There are between 1 and 2 million alligators living in Florida and it might surprise you to know that they don't just live in swamps and marshland. Alligators can be commonly found in lakes, canals, rivers and even ponds. What's more, they can also go walkabout and gators have been found outside homes, under cars and even in swimming pools.

Since documentation on alligator attacks began in 1928, just over 300 unprovoked bites have been recorded to date with 22 of these resulting in fatalities. Alligators tend to be attracted to smaller prey and it's therefore imperative to keep pets and children well away from Florida waters.

I'm told that alligators tend to shy away from humans. Perhaps this is why a number of Floridians use Florida lakes to swim, kayak and go tube riding. Now I don't know whether this is true or not but for what it's worth here's my take on it. There's a pretty good chance that any body of freshwater in Florida contains an alligator. Gators are predators and carnivores and can grow to over 14 feet in length. For those that swim in Florida lakes and retrieve their golf ball at the edge of their water hazard, I say good luck to them - I'm too fond of my limbs to do things like that.

The following safety tips regarding alligators are provided by the Florida Fish and Wildlife Conservation Commission:

istockphoto/borsheim

1. Generally, alligators less than 4 ft in length are not large enough to be dangerous unless handled. However, if you encounter any alligator that you believe poses a threat to people, pets or property, call the nuisance alligator hotline at 866-392-4286.

2. Be aware of the possibility of alligators when you are in or near fresh or brackish water. Bites may occur when people do not pay close enough attention to their surroundings when working or recreating near water.

3. Do not swim outside of posted swimming areas or in waters that might be inhabited by large alligators.

4. Alligators are most active between dusk and dawn. Therefore avoid swimming at night.

5. Dogs and cats are similar in size to the natural prey of alligators. Don't allow pets to swim, exercise or drink in or near waters that may contain alligators. Dogs often attract an alligator's interest, so do not swim with your dog.

6. Leave alligators alone. State law prohibits killing, harassing or possessing alligators. Handling even small alligators can result in injury.

7. Never feed alligators – it's dangerous and illegal. When fed, alligators can overcome their natural wariness and learn to associate people with food. When this happens, some of these alligators have to be removed and killed.

8. Dispose of fish scraps in garbage cans at boat ramps and fish cans. Do not throw them into the water. Although you are not intentionally feeding alligators when you do this, the result can be the same.

9. Seek immediate medical attention if you are bitten by an alligator. Alligator bites can result in serious infection.

10. Observe and photograph alligators only from a distance.

Spiders

In Britain I only ever came across the traditional harmless house spider or equally tame daddy long legs. Although I'm not particularly fond of them, I was always able to muster up enough courage to re-locate them out of my home if I was in a particularly caring mood, or kill them off with a good old whack with a shoe if I was having a bad day. Now living in Florida, I inspect any discovered spiders in my home, garden or mailbox a lot more carefully before attempting removal.

The majority of Florida spiders are not harmful to humans but there are five species of venomous ones. These are: the Southern Black Widow, Northern Black Widow, Red Widow, Brown Widow and Brown Recluse. Widow spiders are identifiable by their coloured hourglass markings on the underside of their abdomen (with the exception of the red Widow which usually has one or two small red marks instead).

The fifth venomous spider is the Brown Recluse. It is light tan to deep reddish-brown in colour and has a distinctive dark violin-shaped mark on its head and thorax. Anyone bitten by any of these five spiders should immediately seek medical assistance.

Snakes

Snakes are also on my list of least favorite things that I like to meet. It doesn't matter how many times people tell me that they are good to have around, how they help with the eco-system and how useful they are at eating rodents and other pest type creatures, I'm still not convinced.

There are approximately 45 different species of snakes in Florida but thankfully only 6 of these types are venomous. These dangerous six are; the Cottonmouth, Southern Copperhead, Eastern Diamondback, Eastern Coral Snake, Timber Rattlesnake and the Dusky Pigmy.

Snakes come in many shapes, size, markings and colours. The colours of some species can also change as the snake grows from youth into adulthood. Unless you have a good background of snakes and can easily identify them as the venomous or non-venomous variety (and I suggest that as a Brit you don't have that expert knowledge!), they should not be approached.

One of the most common types of snake that is seen around Florida is the 'Black Racer'. In their youth, they are actually brown in colour, but as adults, turn black with white markings in the chin area. They are known to inhabit both rural and urban places and are frequently seen in residential areas during the daytime. Racers (hence the name!) are fast movers and will usually flee if come across, but can bite in an attempt to defend themselves. They may be harmless, but as with all snakes, I'm still giving them a wide berth.

Florida Pests

If you desire to live in a sub-tropical climate then you must also accept that you will be encountering some unpleasant pests and insects too on your daily travels. Unless your family doesn't mind sharing the bathroom with the odd cockroach or two, enlisting a pest control service to take care of your home is money very well spent.

Ants

There are a wide variety of ants that can be found in Florida and one of their most annoying features is to be able to find entry into your home. If you're not careful food crumbs or sticky substances such as left over apple juice can lead to a trail of black ants to that location the next day.

Additionally, there is a particularly harmful species of ant in Florida which is commonly encountered. They are called 'fire ants'. These types of ants are small, reddish-orange in color and they unfortunately bite. When a person receives such a bite, it resembles a pimple on the skin which can itch for several days. Medical issues can also arise if the victim is subject to several bites or has an allergic reaction to them.

Fire ants typically nest outdoors in small grey dirt mounds. You can often see these mounds anywhere that contains soil, such as your yard or other grassy area. If accidently trodden on, the nest becomes disturbed resulting in fire ants coming out and on the attack. One of the things I miss about Britain is being able to let your children play on the lawn without the worry of potential ant nests.

Mosquitoes

As soon as you arrive in Florida you will notice that many of the homes have screens attached to the rear of them. There's a reason for this. Florida has more species of mosquitoes than any other State. More importantly, they can spread diseases such as St Louis encephalitis, eastern equine encephalitis, and West Nile virus.

Female mosquitoes need blood to develop their eggs and when a mosquito bites, it injects a small amount of anti-coagulant which hastens blood flow. When a person has an allergic reaction to the anti-coagulant, the area swells up or itches. To protect yourself from them wear clothing that covers most of your body, use a mosquito repellent containing DEET, and avoid going out in the early morning, dusk and evening when mosquitoes are most active.

Love Bugs

In the months of April/May and August/September you will find a strange species flying around in the air. Two black skinny earwig type bugs that are joined together by their ends. They are actually black flies (Diptera) with a red thorax and are harmless. Unfortunately, they have a tendency to selfishly fly right into the path of your speeding vehicle and are a real pain to remove from your paintwork and grill.

Black Bears

The Florida Black Bear is the largest land mammal in Florida and it is estimated that there are between 2500 and 3000 of these species living there. They are usually shy and will hide from people but are nevertheless powerful wild animals and can do you some harm if you come across one and it feels threatened. While there have been no recorded predatory bear attacks on people in Florida, people have been bitten and scratched by bears who were defending themselves, their cubs or their food source. The Florida black bear is usually found in the more rural areas of Florida, such as in its many State Parks but they have also been known to venture into residential areas at night on occasions.

The Florida Panther

The Florida Panther is a subspecies of puma. It is estimated that roughly 100-160 of them live in Florida, mostly in the southwest region but there have also been sightings of them further north and even into Georgia. Florida panthers are reclusive, tend to live in remote, undeveloped areas and move primarily at night. It's therefore very rare to see one. There has been no record of a Florida Panther ever attacking a person but in the unlikely event of encountering one, the Florida Fish and Wildlife Conservation Commission advise people to give them space, not run, appear larger and fight back if ever attacked.

Bobcats

Bobcats can be mistaken for a smaller version of the Florida panther. They are the size of a medium sized dog and are typically brown or grey in colour with black spots or streaks and yellow or white undersides. Bobcats get their name from their short 'bobbed' tails and live in forests, rural areas and swamps. They are often seen in these areas but it is uncommon to be attacked by one. Bobcats eat small animals such as rabbits, rats, mice and raccoons.

Wild Pigs

The wild pig, otherwise known as a wild hog, wild boar or feral pig is one of the more nuisance animals that live in the State. They can be found in all counties of Florida and in at least 35 States. It is estimated that there are over 3 million of these animals nationwide, with Florida homing at least half a million of these, only superseded by the state of Texas.

There are two main reasons for their nuisance. Firstly, they often feed by 'rooting', digging for food below the surface of the ground with their broad snouts. This causes disturbances to the soil and ground and damages landscapes, farmers' fields and homeowner lawns. Other damage is often caused by trampling over vegetation and crops and by destroying fencing. Secondly, these animals can also host many diseases and parasites including hog cholera, tuberculosis, brucellosis, ticks, fleas and lice.

Wild hogs are omnivorous which means they eat all kinds of foods, both plants and animals. Acorns are their favourite but they will eat almost anything. They live in a wide variety of habitats but prefer moist forests, swamps and pine flatwoods. Wild hogs can be dangerous as although they prefer to run from danger, they can be very aggressive when they feel threatened and can cause serious injury with their tusks.

Wild pigs are popular animals to hunt and are in fact the second-most popular large animal hunted in Florida, second only to the white-tailed deer. They can be trapped and hunted year round using any legally owned firearm or crossbow and without the need for a hunting licence.

Chapter 5

Driving in Florida

Most of us Brits consider ourselves pretty good drivers. We have years of experience in negotiating windy country roads, bustling city centres and three lane motorways and given the often limited space in Britain, we can usually pull off parking our vehicles in even the smallest of spaces.

Leaving a major airport onto Florida roads for the first time however can often sap that driving confidence right out of you. Unfamiliar road signs, crazy Floridian drivers and the fact that you're driving on what your brain keeps telling you is the wrong side of the road does not make for an easy transition! Fear not. This first major challenge for you will not take long to get used to, although be prepared to embarrass yourself on at least a couple of occasions by getting into the vehicle only to find the steering wheel on the other side.

The Convenience Factor

Many things in the States are very 'convenience' orientated compared to Britain and driving is a very good example of this. The preferred type of vehicle for Floridians to drive are those with automatic transmissions rather than manual ones, and if you are unfamiliar with driving an automatic, this could well be challenge number two for you. Another popular convenient feature is the 'cruise control' which allows the driver to set the vehicle's speed. This is a useful tool particularly on long journeys and to help prevent inadvertent speeding.

You will be familiar with fast food 'Drive Thru's' across Britain. In the States however, Drive Thru's do not just extend to obtaining a burger with fries from the comfort of your vehicle. Drive thrus are also used at non-food establishments such as at banks and pharmacies and are very convenient facilities to have. Even 'drive thru' flu shots have been advertised!

Standards of Driving

There is no amount of money in circulation that could induce me to either walk, cycle or change a tyre at the side of the road in Florida, and here's why. On a regular basis, I will be happily driving to school to drop off my kids for the day or less happily be driving myself to work. Frequently on these occasions, the vehicle in front will begin to veer off the road and onto the grass verge for a few seconds before correcting itself and returning to the tarmac. What causes the driver to do this? Well, here's my hunch:

In the State of Florida, it is not illegal to use your mobile phone whilst driving, and surprisingly this also includes texting. While there have been numerous attempts to bring in legislation prohibiting drivers at the very least texting, nothing has so far been successful, and at the time of writing, Florida remains one of 15 States that do not have laws against using your phone behind the wheel. Additionally, having cruise control and no gear changing to worry about can tempt drivers to carry out other activities whilst driving instead of concentrating on the road.

Safety Laws

Many driving laws in Britain are implemented and enforced in order to protect the personal safety of the individual whether they like it or not. This isn't necessarily true in the State of Florida. Although compulsory in Britain for example, it is not illegal to ride a motorcycle without a helmet in the State as long as they are at least 21 years of age and can provide proof of medical insurance coverage of at least $10,000.

The laws in Florida relating to the wearing of seat belts can also be a little perplexing. Without a seatbelt, you are much more likely to be killed or seriously injured in the event of an accident. Prior to 2009 though, motorists on Florida's roads could only be ticketed for not wearing their seatbelt if they were stopped for another violation. After 2009 legislation brought stricter regulations. Florida law now states (with some exceptions) that all drivers and front seat passengers must wear seatbelts and that all passengers under 18 years of age must wear either a seatbelt or otherwise be restrained by a child car seat.

Although obviously a vast improvement to personal safety, the legislation still does not make it a requirement for any passenger over 18 to wear seatbelts in the rear of vehicles. Nor does the legislation apply to 'a space within a truck body primarily intended for merchandise or property'. This therefore makes it perfectly legal in Florida for people to be driven around in the back of trucks and you will see it often on Florida roads.

Drink Driving

Over recent years drinking and driving in Britain has become increasingly socially unacceptable particularly amongst younger generations. Anyone seen to drink more than one alcoholic drink in the U.K with the intention of driving afterwards is generally looked at with scorn and runs the risk of either being stopped by police routinely on their way home or as a result of someone in the bar making a tip-off to police. The British Government's Drink Driving Campaigns remind people that any amount of alcohol affects your ability to drive and that you run the risk of a fine of up to £5000, a minimum 12 month driving ban and a criminal record.

The State of Florida drink driving laws prohibits anyone over 21 years of age from driving a vehicle with a blood alcohol concentration of 0.8 percent or above. This is the same legal alcohol limit as in the U.K. However the practice of driving after having a beer appears more socially acceptable by Floridians than it is in Britain and since living in the State, I have only met one person so far that will not drink any alcohol if they intend on driving later.

Whether this has something to do with how strict law enforcement is regarding the issue, how it's generally perceived by Americans or how strongly the issue is conveyed by the media, I cannot say, although the slogan for the current drink driving commercial in Florida reminds drivers that 'buzzed' driving is still drunk driving'. Statistically, with a population of just over 18 million people, nearly 800 people died in Florida in 2010 as a result of alcohol related crashes. The same year in

Britain, with its population of over 62 million people, a much lesser amount of 250 people died due to drink driving.

Excess Speed

I may question how safe Florida roads are at times but there is one area of traffic law that law enforcement seem to be well on top of – Speeding. As well as police agencies that patrol their own towns, there exists the 'Florida Highway Patrol' a sort of Statewide Police traffic Department. When they are not dealing with road accidents or other duties, you will often see their dark coloured black and cream vehicles discreetly parked up and on the lookout for speeding violators.

While it may be a common sight in Britain to see vehicles being driven routinely at 90mph on a 70mph limit motorway, be warned - drive more than the 65mph or 70mph speeding limit even on a remote quiet highway in the middle of the night in Florida and you risk receiving an expensive citation. It took me a couple of speeding tickets before I learned that I had to drive much stricter to the speed limits than in the U.K, and despite cursing the FHP all the way home on those expensive occasions, I have to admit that the strict enforcement of speeding laws make Florida roads much safer.

If you do get pulled over by the police in Florida it is important to remain seated in your vehicle unless directed to do otherwise by the officer. The practice of getting out of your vehicle and meeting with the officer may be acceptable in Britain but in the U.S such actions are likely to be interpreted by the officer as confrontational. Unless you want a police gun drawn on you, make sure you remain in the vehicle with your hands clearly visible at all times.

Road Accidents

If you are unfortunately involved in a road accident, you are required by Florida law to do the following:

1. Stop.

2. Get help if anyone is hurt.

3. Provide your name, address and vehicle registration number and show your drivers' license to others involved in the crash.

4. Report to police any vehicle accident that involves injuries or property damage over $500.

5. For a collision with a parked, unattended vehicle, leave a note with your name, address and licence plate and report the accident to police.

Driving Practices unique to the U.S

It is useful to read through the 'Florida Drivers Handbook' prior to obtaining your Florida license. Not only will it help you pass your theory driving test but it also contains some driving rules and regulations that may be unfamiliar to a British driver new to American roads as they are not practiced in Britain. Here are three as an example;

<u>Turning Right on Red</u>: After stopping at a red traffic light, you may turn right on red at most intersections if the way is clear. Some intersections display a 'No turn on red" sign, which you must obey.

<u>School Bus Stop law Requirements</u>: Florida motor vehicle laws require that motorists stop upon approaching any school bus (these are bright yellow in colour) which displays its flashing red lights and has its stop signs extended.

Istockphoto/EdwardShackleford

<u>Stop Signs</u>: Stop signs are octagonal. A stop sign means that you must bring your vehicle to a complete halt at the marked stop line. If there is no marked stop line, stop before entering the crosswalk on the near side of the intersection. A four way stop sign means that there are four stop signs at this intersection, and traffic from all four directions must stop. The first vehicle to reach the intersection should move forward first. If two vehicles reach the intersection at the same time, the driver on the left yields to the driver on the right.

Chapter 6

Food & Drink

Now you may think that food is relatively similar both in Britain and in the United States but that's not necessarily so. It may be the same type of food but the taste can be a lot different than what you're used to. Changing what you have eaten all your life can be quite a challenging thing to do. You may have grown up with Walkers Crisps, Walls sausages, Mcvities biscuits and Cadbury chocolate, but now they're no longer on the shelves of your local store. American aisles are still filled with bags of crisps and chocolate of course, but they can have a slightly different flavor than what you may be used to.

Grocery Stores

Upon arrival, you will find your local supermarket full of unfamiliar foods and brands to explore. It may take a while (and some cash!) to find foods that appeal to your palette or were similar to what you used to eat back home. For those that just can't do without some of their favourite British comfort foods, you will be pleased to know that some of the most popular British brands can be found in the 'ethnic' or 'international' aisle of leading supermarkets or at various British shops located in Florida. These supermarket sections contain items such as; Robinsons orange juice, Smarties chocolate, Bisto gravy and Jacobs crackers. Be warned though, as the marmite you simply can't live without will be in a tiny jar and cost three times as much than what you used to pay back home.

An unfortunate absence in Florida is the online grocery shopping facility. Ordering your weekly items online from stores such as Tescos and Asda to be delivered to your door at a designated date and time was always a particular useful alternative to me back in Britain than negotiating through a busy store with my 2 year old son and newborn daughter on tow.

Unfortunately, this facility isn't available from any of the large chain of Florida supermarkets. The only consolation to this is that thanks to Florida's laid back lifestyle, visiting the supermarket is usually a little more relaxing than it ever was back in Britain. Stores tend to be less crowded and more convenient with staff usually very friendly and willing to help you. Groceries are packed for you at checkout and some stores even carry your bags out to your vehicle for you at no extra charge. As an added bonus, free cookies are handed out to children, a marvelous idea to keep them quiet for a while!

Restaurants

America is of course famous for its fast food restaurants. Some of them such as Mcdonalds, Burger King and KFC we are already familiar with, but the U.S has many others. A wide variety of food can be found at these establishments from Chinese and Mexican to ice-cream and donuts.

There are also many chains of sit-down restaurants for those in search of a little more quality and a nicer dining environment. Some of the more well-known ones are: Applebee's, T.G.I Fridays, Olive Garden and Chili's. Alcohol is usually available in these types of restaurants and soft drinks are often refilled at no extra charge.

Portion sizes are much larger than back in Britain so it's uncommon to be able to eat all three courses. You are usually offered a Styrofoam box or 'doggy bag' so that you can take left over food home with you. After receiving your check (bill) it is customary to tip your server anywhere between 10-20% of the total price.

Another type of restaurant associated with America is the 'Diner'. Many open 24 hours a day and are popular with locals especially for breakfast. 'Dennys' is one of the more popular chains of diner offering a variety of food at economical prices.

Although the States may be associated with burgers and fries there are many traditional foods that are popular among Americans. They vary by geographical area but popular items include; barbequed meat, fried chicken, apple and key lime pie, corn bread and cheesecake. Holidays such as Thanksgiving and Halloween also generate seasonal items such as pumpkin pie.

Quenching your Thirst

Coffee houses have become very popular over recent years. 'Starbucks' is one of the most famous and offers a variety of coffee related beverages including smoothies and iced drinks. Many of these stores have 'drive thru' facilities for added convenience.

There may not be a pub on every corner but there are still a wide variety of bars on offer. The minimum drinking age is 21 and photo I.D is often required when purchasing. Popular domestic beers on offer include; Budweiser, Miller, Cools and Busch. To buy alcohol for home consumption, beer and wine can be purchased in supermarkets, but other types of alcohol are generally only obtained by visiting a liquor store.

Chapter 7

Education

Trying to keep a handle on your child's development in school can be a difficult enough task as it is, but throw a different education system than what your used to into the equation and you could well be left scratching your head in confusion. Forget finishing school at 16 years of age, GCSE exams and 6 week summer holidays. Here's how America does things:

Grades

Although it can vary by State, children usually begin schooling at the age of 5 in America and typically finish High School at the age of 18. They are divided by age groups into 'Grades' ranging from Kindergarten in their 1st year up to 12th Grade in their final year. Kids will often inform you which grade they are in and until my children started school, it meant absolutely nothing to me. The following is a useful chart on the school grading system so that when it happens to you, you won't have to stare blankly at the child like I did.

PRE-SCHOOL	AGE:
Pre-Kindergarten (VPK)	4-5

ELEMENTARY SCHOOL	AGE:
Kindergarten	5-6
1st Grade	6-7
2nd Grade	7-8
3rd Grade	8-9
4th Grade	9-10
5th Grade	10-11

MIDDLE SCHOOL	AGE:
6th Grade	11-12
7th Grade	12-13
8th Grade	13-14

HIGH SCHOOL	AGE:
9TH Grade (Freshman)	14-15
10th Grade (Sophomore)	15-16
11th Grade (Junior)	16-17
12th Grade (Senior)	17-18

The Academic Year

The U.S school year is generally shorter than the U.K. It usually begins in late August, finishing the following year in June. It is typically broken into two semesters; one in the fall and one in spring. Children are typically given two weeks break over Christmas and a week off around March called 'Spring Break'. Schools will also be closed during several public holidays such as Labor Day, Memorial Day and Thanksgiving.

Summer Camps

The length of the academic year means that kids get well over 2 months for their summer holidays. Two months is a long time to occupy children, even with an Xbox 360 in the home. It can also prove particularly difficult when both parents may be working full time.

A popular solution for many parents are 'Summer Camps'. Many organizations offer a week of activities for children to partake in during their summer vacation period. These activities range from a variety of sports such as soccer, karate, tennis and horse riding, to educational activities at places like museums, art centres and local zoos. Even some of the theme parks offer camps such as Orlando Seaworld and the Kennedy Space Center.

Summer Camps are a great way to keep your kids busy and many have the added benefit of teaching them new skills. Babysitting your children with activities thrown in comes at a price though and fees to enroll your child in these camps can be expensive depending on the activities and organization you select.

Assessment

Upon completing high school, children in Britain receive GCSE qualifications based on examinations and coursework for each subject that they have taken. In the U.S however, students instead work towards completing a 'High School Diploma'.

Students are generally assessed continuously throughout the academic year and given a final grade at the end of each semester. These grades are averaged over the student's high school years to produce a Grade Point Average (GPA). They may also receive a class rank which shows how their GPA fairs in comparison to their peers. Receiving a High School Diploma shows that the student has successfully completed secondary education to the required State level. It is given to them at a High School graduation ceremony where students are dressed in cap and gown and called forward individually to receive their Diploma. Having a high school diploma is essential to continue with Higher Education and is often required to enter many careers.

General Educational Development (GED)

For any adult who does not hold a High School Diploma and wishes to obtain such a qualification, the U.S offers the 'General Education Development' Test. It's a test consisting of 5 subjects; Science, Maths, Social Studies, Language Arts – writing and Language Arts- Reading. When passed, it certifies that the holder has American

High School-level academic skills. It is often taken by people who have immigrated as an adult into the country, have left high school early or was unsuccessful at passing their High School Diploma during their school years.

Because of its multiple choice format, there has been some dispute as to whether the GED test is easier than a High School Diploma. It is due to be changed into two levels: one for students wanting the GED as a high school equivalency qualification and to assist them with entering the job market. The second level will be for those students wishing to attend University.

Voluntary Pre-Kindergarten Education VPK

The State of Florida provides a free educational program to all 4 year old children. It's called Voluntary Pre-Kindergarten Education (VPK). It focuses on reading, writing and social skills and prepares children to be ready for Kindergarten.

VPK is free to all Florida residents who have a child turning 4 years of age by September 1st. Parents get to choose which participating facility to enroll their child in and also have some options on the child's hours of attendance, for example every weekday morning or every weekday afternoon. The program makes pre-school children better prepared for Kindergarten and also provides parents of 4 year olds with some State qualified childcare for free!

University Education

University is called College in the U.S. Courses are typically four years in length and like High school, the four Undergraduate grades are called freshman, sophomore, junior and senior.

Perhaps the biggest difference in higher education in the States compared to Britain is the cost involved. Although University education is no longer free in Britain, the amount that a student (or parent!) is expected to contribute is significantly less than in the U.S. The U.S College Board reported that a moderate college budget for an in-state public college for 2011-2012 academic year averaged $21,447 and at a private college averaged $42,224 per academic year. That's a lot of dough for a parent to find for a 4 year degree program and that's just for one child.

In some cases, a child's academic, artistic, athletic or other ability could grant them a scholarship. Receiving a scholarship means that financial aid is given to the student in order to further their education. For the rest of us without such gifted children, parents who can afford to do so, can save regular amounts over their children's school years into a College Savings Fund.

Chapter 8

American Healthcare

As much as I liked having a free health service in Britain, it wasn't without its faults. I still remember my father receiving an eye injury from a gardening accident and having to wait 14 hours to be treated in A & E one night. I was also decidedly unimpressed to be told during labour that I couldn't have my planned epidural due to staff shortages. Free healthcare is a wonderful thing provided you still receive a decent level of service and aren't on a nine month waiting list for an operation when you have only been given six months to live.

After living in a country that provides free healthcare, the American system can take some adjusting to. The first thing to understand is that many health care providers in the United States are for- profit organizations and are in the business of making money. The second thing to make clear is that American healthcare is very, very expensive. How expensive? Well, in 2007, over half of all bankruptcy filings in the U.S were due to medical bills. *That* expensive.

According to the Institute of Medicine of the National Academy of Sciences, the United States is the only wealthy, industrialized nation that does not have a universal health care system. Health insurance is available to protect yourself from large medical expenses and in 2010 approximately 84% of Americans had some type of health insurance in place.

Medical Insurance

Medical insurance often comes in one of three ways:

Individual

You can purchase health insurance directly from a private health insurer. This is usually an expensive option and you may need to accept a high excess amount in order to keep monthly insurance premiums affordable. Only 9% of the 84% of insured Americans have coverage in this way, but if you're self-employed or your employer doesn't offer any health benefits then this may be the only option available to you.

Employer Provided

Almost 60% of health insurance coverage in America is provided by an employer. Employers typically cover a large portion of the monthly premium and then the employee must contribute the remaining amount. With a member of the family in full time employment, medical coverage can often extend not just to the employee themselves, but also to their spouse and children as well.

Now the problem with having your health insurance through your employer is the effect it has when you change your employment status. If an American loses their job, seeks alternative employment or takes a career break to raise a family they could well become medically uninsured. Additionally, the rising costs of health care make it increasingly more difficult for employers to provide it to their employees, and some will opt to hire part time or freelance workers instead in order to avoid having to pay healthcare benefits.

Government Related

The Government also covers medical insurance for the elderly, Federal employees, the military, the disabled and for some people on low income. There are several Government funded programs:

Medicare:

Medicare provides health insurance for the elderly and to certain disabled Americans. The program is categorized into parts. Part A covers hospital care including nursing facilities. Part B covers outpatient care, doctor services and preventive care. Part C is the Medicare Advantage Plan, custom health plans for individuals, and Part D helps cover the cost of prescription drugs. The individual will still need to pay their deductible for any medical services provided.

To be eligible for the program, you must be at least 65 years of age or be under 65 with certain disabilities. You also need to have been a U.S Citizen or permanent legal resident (green card holder) for at least five continuous years and be eligible for social security benefits by making at least 10 years of social security payments (similar to our British National Insurance payments).

Medicaid:

Medicaid provides health insurance for low income individuals and families. Although it's a Federal Government program each State runs its own Medicaid program and determines eligibility and services offered. Some services, such as hospital, prenatal, pediatric and physician services are mandatory for States to provide.

The program is primarily for people with low incomes but eligibility can also depend on age, assets, pregnancy, disability and citizen or immigrant status.

The State Children's Health Insurance:

This program was created in 1997. It provides health insurance to uninsured children whose families earn too much income to qualify for Medicaid but not enough income to be able to purchase private health insurance. It provides coverage for such things as: hospital care, doctor and dental visits and prescription drugs. Similar to Medicaid, each State runs its own program with its own eligibility rules.

American Healthcare Issues

Many Americans believe that their current healthcare system needs reform. Medical services in America are some of the best in the world, with advanced technology available and minimal waiting times for treatment compared to many other countries. However health insurance is not affordable to many and over 47 million Americans are uninsured.

Many are able to afford health insurance because it is subsidized by their employer but the link between employment and health care can have a negative effect on both employers footing the bill and individuals changing their employment status. Some argue that a person's medical insurance should belong and travel with the individual themselves and have no affiliation with their job at all.

Under the Emergency Medical Treatment and Labor Act no-one can be turned away for medical treatment in the event of a medical emergency. Many without insurance end up waiting until they are brought into the Emergency Room in order to be treated. Some argue that this costs the system much more than if they had been given preventative or routine treatment to begin with. It also overburdens Emergency Rooms and further impacts them financially.

Ultimately, the U.S spends more per capita than any other nation in the world but as per the Institute of medicine, it's 'among the few industrialized nations in the world that does not guarantee access to health care for its population'. Methods for reform will continue to be debated by Government and others for some time to come.

Chapter 9

Money Matters

Many wonder whether the cost of living in Florida is any cheaper than living in Britain and it's a difficult question to answer. To a British tourist, many goods for sale in Florida appear relatively inexpensive, leading many to return home with a suitcase full of new clothes and other items that they've purchased at 'bargain' prices.

However, it is important to remember that these prices are often only attractive because of their British wage and a strong pound to the dollar exchange rate. Living in Florida can put a new perspective on things.

The Cost of Living

Typical salaries in Florida can often range between $25,000 - $50,000 per year and the cost of living can take a large portion of that hard earned cash. No State income tax and substantially low prices for petrol compared to the U.K are a refreshing change but living in Florida comes with other expenditure that can balance out the cost of living scales between the U.S and the U.K. The following expenses are things to be aware of:

Electricity:
A hot and humid environment means that air-conditioning in homes is a necessity. Cooling your house 24 hours a day, particularly in the summer months can often produce electricity bills averaging around $200-$350 per month depending on the size of your home. Additionally, houses with swimming pools also use electricity in order to run pool pumps for several hours each day.

Lawns:
The hot climate means that lawns need frequent water in order to survive. Irrigation systems are often used in Florida to maintain a homeowner's garden and watering it several times a week can produce water bills of around $100 per month. Grass grows quickly in the heat and needs frequent cuts. Many homeowners are discouraged from mowing the lawn themselves because of the heat and employ a lawn service instead. The cost for these landscaping services usually cost between $60-100 per month.

Health Insurance:
Healthcare in the United States is not free and health insurance is expensive. The cheapest way to obtain health insurance is by getting it through your employer. They often pay for a large portion of the premium with the employee paying the remaining amount. However even with employer assistance, insurance premiums can still cost a family a few hundred dollars each month. Without employer assistance, a basic health insurance premium for a healthy family of four can often be at least $400 per month and come with high excess amounts of over $10,000.

Vehicle Insurance
Americans have a reputation for frequent litigation and it has an adverse effect on many insurance premiums. Such is the case with car insurance. Even with a good driver record and an average family car, insurance premiums can cost around $100 per month.

Banking

For a nation that's put a man on the moon, banking in the United States can be a bit of a letdown. We are used to carrying out our banking online with electronic payments and direct debits an ordinary and everyday occurrence. In America however, many of the banks' online facilities are fairly limited in comparison. Most don't allow you to transfer money online directly into other people's accounts or set up, amend or cancel direct debit or standing order payments at the touch of a few buttons.

Additionally, many banks in the U.S charge fees for various services which we would expect to be free in the U.K. Opening up an account for example, may provide you with an ATM/debit card but you are likely to be charged if you want a cheque book to come with it. And it's not as if a cheque book is a redundant item – Americans use cheques regularly to pay for services, bills and even rent. Wages are also often given by cheque although the direct deposit method is gaining in popularity. Many employees are also paid on a weekly or bi-weekly basis rather than monthly.

Given that a lot of banking can't be done online, it is at least a comfort that visiting a bank in America is usually a little nicer and more convenient than in the U.K. Back in Britain, if I wanted to make a deposit, I needed to drive to into my local town, find a place to park my vehicle, take a walk to the High Street and locate the bank. In the U.S, banks are easy to visit by car, with plenty of parking and 'drive thru' facilities so that you can make deposits and remove money from ATMs without even having to leave your vehicle. For visits inside the bank, coffee and sometimes even biscuits are usually on offer while you wait.

Credit Issues

No matter how great your credit score was in the U.K, your U.S credit when you first arrive will look decidedly bleak. No credit history in the U.S can be both annoying and problematic. It can hinder important purchases such as buying a home or purchasing a car and make you pay much higher deposits than others for items and services like mobile phones and utilities. That's not to say that you will always be refused credit, but any approval you receive is likely to come with a large interest rate attached.

There are ways to build your credit but it will take time. Some finance providers and banks offer a credit card providing you pay the full credit limit amount up front. Other ways are to apply for store cards. Although the limit will be very minimal, it can give you the opportunity to show a pattern of making good monthly payments. It may take a few years to build your credit history but providing you don't fall behind or make late payments, your credit score will continue to rise so that in time, you will no longer be so disadvantaged.

The Currency

It may look like monopoly money to you but you will soon learn to get used to it. Make sure that you become familiar with the currency quite quickly so that you can identify amounts easily. Handing over a $100 bill instead of a $20 one will make you go broke very quickly and holding out a handful of coins for the cashier to select is just a little embarrassing.

Taxes

Florida is one of seven States that doesn't have personal income tax. It's one of the reasons why Florida has one of the lowest tax burdens in the country. Individuals are still required however to pay Federal taxes and also social security contributions (similar to National insurance payments).

Sales tax is similar to what we know back in Britain as VAT or value added tax, except it's cheaper. The State charges a 6% tax on the sale or rental of goods with some exceptions. The difference (apart from the percentage rate) is that the sales tax is added on to the price at the point of purchase. You might therefore buy an item with a dollar price tag but get charged $1.06 by the cashier. Additionally, some Florida counties impose a local tax on items of around 1.5%.

Filing Annual Tax Returns

In Britain, people aren't often required to fill in tax returns. Income tax and National insurance contributions are automatically taken out of the person's wages according to their salary and it's up to the individuals to apply to the Inland Revenue for any exemption or child benefit that may be available to them. Tax returns are required in Britain when a person receives some other form of income such as those who receive money through property rental or the self-employed.

In the U.S however, all U.S citizens and residents who earn more than the statutory minimum amount of gross income are required to file an annual tax return to the Internal Revenue Service (IRS). Upon employment, individuals complete a Form W-4 called an 'Employee's Withholding Allowance Certificate'. On the form, the employee states their personal details, including social security number and number of dependants. An estimated amount of tax is then taken from their pay cheque based on this information.

At the beginning of each year, American workers receive a Form 'W-2' from their employer which details the amount of gross income received by the employee and the amount of tax withheld. The taxpayer then fills in their tax return on a 'Form 1040' using these figures and claiming for any tax credits available to them such as child benefits, healthcare payments and the total amount of interest paid on their mortgage.

The annual deadline to file the Federal individual income tax return is April 15th although extensions can be applied for. Many companies also provide services to complete the tax return for you. After completion, the tax return shows whether the taxpayer still owes the IRS any taxes or if the individual has paid too much tax over the course of the previous year. In cases of overpayment, a refund in the form of a cheque is then mailed to the individual. Many Americans receive cheques from the IRS at this time of the year and it's a tempting time to make some lavish purchases.

Chapter 10

Crime, Guns & Bad Behavior

Maybe it has something to do with the Hollywood movies, their heavy military responses, the old Wild West or their right to bear arms, but Americans do have a bit of a reputation for their guns and the violence associated with them.

For a Brit, arriving in the United States can therefore be quite a culture shock. We have been brought up in a country that is relatively gun free and where even the majority of our police officers carry out their duties unarmed. This does not mean of course that Britain is without its share of violence. With limited access to firearms, violent crimes are instead committed using alternative weapons such as knives, baseball bats or just by way of an old fashioned beating.

Nevertheless, it can still lead a Brit to question what exactly they have got themselves into after arriving in the U.S and hearing stories of shootings on their local news. So, are the streets regularly a scene from the O.K Corral? Do all Americans carry a bulge under their jacket and just how violent is Florida with so many firearms in existence?

The Right to Bear Arms

The majority of Americans have the right to own a gun. It comes from the Second Amendment of the United States Constitution which speaks of 'the right of the people to keep and bear Arms'. Those currently excluded from owning them include; convicted felons, illegal aliens, the mentally ill, those under court restraining orders and unlawful users of controlled substances.

Surveys estimate that just less than 50% of the population owns a firearm. The main reasons given for their possession are for protection from crime but other reasons include target shooting and for hunting purposes. Gun laws vary by State and this Chapter will concentrate on the current laws relating to Florida. Additionally, since the tragic shootings at Sandy Hook Elementary school in Newtown, Connecticut, gun laws in the U.S are currently under review.

Possessing a Firearm

In the State of Florida, buyers do not need to register their firearms or obtain a licence in order to own one. If they have purchased the weapon from a licensed dealer, they must submit to a background check (this is a Federal Law) but background checks are not currently required if they have been purchased either from a gun show or privately between individuals. At the time of writing, President Obama is attempting to change legislation and impose universal background checks as well as making efforts to re-instate a ban on assault weapons. However, in order to achieve this he needs approval from Congress which is no easy task.

In Florida, those who wish to carry a gun in public can do so if it's concealed and the holder has first obtained a 'concealed carry' licence. Applicants for such a license must be over 21, complete one of the accepted forms of gun training and will be denied if they fall into any of the exclusions (such as being a convicted felon, show a dependence on alcohol or drugs or be subject to a domestic violence injunction). Even with the concealed permit, there are still areas that you are not permitted to carry in public, such as in a school, bar, police station or courthouse.

Guns may be stored in vehicles in the State of Florida without the need of a licence but they must be securely encased and not readily accessible. The person in possession of the firearm is also required to be at least eighteen years of age. It is also illegal to discharge a firearm whilst intoxicated and to shoot in a public place unless in self defence.

Florida's 'Stand Your Ground' Law

In Florida, there is something known as 'Stand your Ground Law'. It entitles a person to defend themselves using deadly force if need be, if they face the threat of death or great bodily harm and are in a place where they are lawfully entitled to be.

The law came under the spotlight in 2011 in Sanford, Florida. A neighbourhood watch volunteer by the name of George Zimmerman phoned 911 to report a suspicious black teenager wearing a hoody loitering in the neighbourhood. The operator asked Zimmerman, who was a 28 year old Hispanic male, if he was following the individual and when he replied 'yes', she told him 'you don't need to do that'. The neighbourhood watch volunteer nevertheless followed the individual and a confrontation ensued.

Upon arrival, police discovered the unarmed youth by the name of Trayvon Martin shot and killed and police reported that Zimmerman had injuries to his face. Zimmerman alleged that he was attacked by Martin and had to use deadly force in order to defend himself. He was subsequently arrested for second degree murder. The incident has received huge media coverage and his trial is due to commence in the summer of 2013.

'10-20-LIFE'

Florida has some of the harshest punishments for gun crime in the nation. In 1999, legislation introduced minimum mandatory prison sentences for offenders who commit crimes with guns. It's often referred to as the '10-20-LIFE' law and it is claimed to have driven down Florida's violent gun crime rates by 30% since its introduction.

Provided by The Florida Department of Corrections

Under the law, mandatory prison sentences are as follows:

Convicted Felon in possession of a firearm = 3 years.

Carrying a gun whilst committing a felony = 10 years.

Firing a gun whilst committing a felony   = 20 years.

Inflicting great harm or death with a firearm during the course of a felony   = min 25 years – life.

Despite its successful results, the law has come under criticism particularly for circumstances where 'warning shots' have been fired. One such controversial case happened in Jacksonville, Florida in 2010. Marissa Alexander, who had a restraining order against her estranged husband, entered the marital home in order to collect her belongings, mistakenly believing her husband to be absent. An argument ensued between them, leading her to enter the garage, retrieve a gun from her car and re-enter the home. Armstrong fired a shot that went into the wall beside her husband. She alleged that her actions were a warning shot in an attempt to get her estranged husband to leave the premises.

Alexander gambled and rejected a plea deal for aggravated assault in which she would have received a 3 year sentence. On trial, the mother of 3 was convicted and received a 20 year prison sentence due to the 10-20-life policy.

Harm vs Benefit

According to a 1994 survey by the U.S Centers for Disease Control and Prevention, Americans use guns to frighten away intruders breaking into their homes about 498,000 times a year. A 1982 survey conducted on male felons reported that:

- 34% had been 'scared off, shot at, wounded, or captured by an armed victim'.
- 40% had decided not to commit a crime because they 'knew or believed that the victim was carrying a gun'.
- 69% personally knew other criminals who had been 'scared off, shot at, wounded or captured by an armed victim'.

Statistics provided by the U.S Centers for Disease Control and Prevention state there were 606 fatal firearm accidents and 14,161 non-fatal firearm accidents in 2010 in the U.S, for a population of 308,745,538. In the same year, the number of murders in the U.S by use of a firearm was reported as 11,078.

Crime & Bad Behavior

The State of Florida is not without its fair share of crime. Figures of course vary depending on the geographical area, with large metropolitan areas such as Miami and Orlando producing much higher reports. The table below shows 2010 and 2011 crime figures for the State which has a population of just over 18 million. These figures have been taken from the Florida Department of Law Enforcement.

OFFENCE	2010	2011
Murder (using firearm)	987 (669)	985 (691)
Sexual Offences	9,886	9,880
Robbery	26,074	25,617
Aggravated Assault	64,960	61,701
Burglary	169,000	170,223
Theft (Larceny)	458,178	461,455
Vehicle Theft	41,433	39,619

While living in a crime free area is certainly desirable, it is unfortunately unrealistic. There will always be neighourhoods considered 'good' and 'bad' and a little research goes a long way when choosing a place to live.

Having made the move, I can now afford to live in a much nicer area than I did back in the U.K. After 5 years of carelessly leaving my vehicle insecure and kids' toys in the front garden I have so far fortunately not yet been relieved of anything. I also remain constantly amazed by the common practice here of postmen leaving parcels on doorsteps. They certainly wouldn't still be there when the owner returns home in my U.K neighbourhood.

Firearms may be easy to obtain and there are certainly areas where I would feel uneasy wandering into during the day let alone by night. Nevertheless, I still feel safer in Florida than back in Britain. The anti-social behavior, so common place in the U.K is distinctly absent. No more abusive youths hanging around on street corners.

No more hooded kids out to pick a fight with anyone in their vicinity, regardless of age. Instead, I'm met with a young generation brought up in an American society and taught to be respectful to their elders. It's a refreshing and welcome change.

Binge drinking is another ugly side of British culture. Young adults spilling out in the early hours onto town centre streets, collapsing or on the look out for a fight. Do Florida streets display the same characteristics? Not even close. Police visibility is much higher and they have a much more no-nonsense approach. It's also illegal for anyone to consume alcohol under the age of 21 and identification is often requested from anyone buying liquor that looks up to the age of 40.

One must always exercise a sensible approach and good judgment in order to minimize your chances of being a victim of crime. This is true wherever you live in the world and nowhere is crime free. Despite its reputation though, I feel more confident to venture out than I ever did back home and I'm glad to be rid of a British society tarnished by anti-social behavior.

Chapter 11

The People

Let's face it, Americans are not the most popular people on the planet. In fact, with their reputation for being loud, armed and arrogant, I'm not sure how many folks would have the United States on their 'places to visit' list if it wasn't for Disney.

In our defence, it's hard to form a positive opinion about American people after watching an episode of the Jerry Springer Show. But do they really live up to their reputation? Well, after 5 years of living and working amongst them, I'm here to put your mind at ease.

I'm quite fond of Americans. I've always found them to be very friendly and welcoming towards me despite my foreign status and unsociable nature. Contrary to popular belief, most of the people I've met have possessed a great sense of humor and can understand my attempts at sarcastic wit just fine. Register Clerks chatting to their customers (even though the queue is getting steadily longer!) and the famous line of 'have a nice day' may be annoying to my mother whenever she visits but I'd take that any day over just being blanked and feeling like an unwanted number back in Britain.

Community Spirit

Americans tend to be more community orientated than back in the U.K. People are generally more neighbourly and more willing to volunteer at their local schools and in their communities. Neighbourhoods regularly put on community events such as Easter egg hunts or Halloween costume parades, and initiatives to help others less fortunate such as food drives or goodwill donations are a common occurrence.

Family Gatherings

Get-togethers between family and friends is an important way of life in the U.S. Seasonal events such as Thanksgiving, Christmas, Halloween parties and 4th J^{uly} celebrations bring family and friends together regularly throughout the year. The practice is also adopted for major sporting events. American Football's Annual Championship game 'the Super bowl' is watched by many Americans at a family or friend's home hosting a 'Super bowl Party' rather than at local bars.

Those Notorious American Traits

Americans do have a couple of traits that if you can learn to live with you will do just fine! They are a very proud nation and you are likely to hear on a regular basis that not only is the U.S a great country but that it is in fact the greatest country on earth. Their steadfast beliefs may originate from their patriotism, upbringing, the U.S media or a mixture of all three but the general consensus is that all other countries are a tad inferior and it gives them their 'arrogant' image. Now, I don't know enough about other countries to make such a determination and the U.S is certainly not without its problems. In all honesty though, maybe they're right – you wouldn't be immigrating to the United States if you didn't think it was half decent now would you?!

Trait No. 2 is that many Americans have very little knowledge about the world outside of the U.S and it produces their reputation as 'ignorant'. Now, this trait isn't necessarily a bad thing for you. For one thing, it makes you look in comparison really smart, cultured and an excellent player in a game of Trivial Pursuit with your State side friends. Discovering that someone doesn't know their Italy from their Australia or to be asked who Tony Blair is may come as a surprise to you but there are two things that you need to bear in mind:

Firstly, the United States is a vast area. There is more than enough newsworthy events to concentrate on in their own local area, State and then Country without broadcasting about places in Europe or other continents that are in reality nothing but distant lands to the average American.

Secondly, Americans really have no need to venture out of their own country except during the course of their employment. Those looking to vacation can find geographical diversity and whatever climate they desire from the fifty States that they can travel freely and relatively inexpensively to. They have beaches in Hawaii and Florida, skiing resorts in Colorado and Vermont, the Deserts of Utah and Nevada, and the big and bustling cities of New York, Las Vegas and Los Angeles. Americans really have no need to go international unless they have a desire for European flavour, foreign language, have a healthy bank account and a fondness for long haul flights. Taking this into consideration, I kind of forgive them for finding the rest of the world a bit of a blur.

Patriotism

I mentioned earlier that Americans display a great amount of pride in their homeland and I find their patriotism particularly admirable. I wish the same level of pride, community spirit and sense of belonging existed in Britain. We may find some traditions a little unorthodox but they undoubtedly play a big part in building a nation loyal and patriotic to their country.

As an example, every morning in American schools children are encouraged to recite the 'Pledge of Allegiance'. It's an expression of loyalty to the Federal Flag and the Republic of the United States of America and has been a long time American tradition. The following is said standing to attention, facing the American flag and with the right hand over the heart:

"I pledge allegiance to the Flag of the United States of America and to the Republic for which it stands, one Nation under God, indivisible, with liberty and justice for all."

Istockphoto/JBryson

When the British National Anthem of 'God save the Queen' is played, do our hearts swell with pride? No, we sit impatiently waiting for the song to finish and slightly embarrassed that it's not a little more upbeat. Now compare that to the U.S. When their National Anthem of 'The Star Spangled Banner' begins, Americans rise, remove headgear and place their hands over their hearts for the duration of the song. The Anthem is played frequently at the beginning of many sporting events, concerts and other public gatherings and the music, lyrics and response from the crowd brings a lump to my throat every time and I'm not even American!

Military Service

Americans have great respect for the military in the U.S, much more so than in the U.K. Military personnel are viewed as vital protectors of the United States and ones who make incredible sacrifices for both their country and for the liberty of American civilians. They often wear their uniform in public and I've seen them being ushered to the front of a line and having their meals and drinks bought for them by members of the public as a mark of respect and gratitude for their service. The Federal Government as well as many other employers provide a 'Veterans Preference' program whereby former service members, including those with a disability, are given an edge over civilian job seekers for employment.

The 'Melting Pot'

Immigration in the U.K has always been a sensitive subject. There has always been much debate and concern over whether Britain was a 'soft touch' and was allowing foreigners into the country who were attracted to British welfare benefits. It's created a lot of animosity towards British immigrants and concern over strains in public services and a loss of 'British' identity.

The U.S however doesn't have such fierce opposition. The country has been built on immigrants migrating to the States in search of a better life for themselves and their family for centuries. American history is filled with such stories from the Pilgrims landing in Massachusetts in 1620 to Ellis Island, New York around the turn of the 20th Century.

People are considered first and foremost as 'Americans' regardless of origin, background and culture. That can't be said for Britain. In 1921 the English philosopher G.K Chesterton visited America and described the U.S as *'the experiment of a democracy of diverse races which has been compared to a melting-pot''.* The U.S is not without its social problems of course but legal immigrants in search of 'the American Dream' are generally welcomed.

If you're worried about how you will be received by Americans don't be. Providing you don't knock their Country or bleat about missing all things British, you are in for some good times and some great company.

Chapter 12

American Sports

The States has much to offer the avid sports fan. Top favourites among Americans are Baseball, Basketball, American Football and Ice Hockey. As a nation that grew up on soccer, tennis and rugby, it's hardly surprising that most of us Brits don't know our touchdowns from our touchbacks or a two-run homers from a grand slam.

What follows is a brief overview on some of the more popular American sports that you are likely to encounter. The rules of each game have deliberately been omitted for fear of sending you into a deep sleep, but if you want to learn about any game in more detail, just get yourself down to your local sports bar, pull up a chair and watch a televised game.

Baseball

Baseball has been a popular sport in the U.S for well over a century and has been described as America's 'National Pastime'. The game has striking similarities to what we know as 'rounders'. Two teams with 9 players on each, attempt to score more 'runs' than the other team by hitting a ball with their bat and then running around 4 bases laid out in the shape of a diamond.

North America's professional baseball league, the MLB is widely followed and consists of 30 teams, mostly from the States but some also from Canada. The season runs from April through to October and begins with a regular season, followed by play offs. The finale of the season is the 'World Series' an annual championship held in October, where the winner is deemed 'world champion'. Yes, I know it's not really 'the world' but that's Americans for you!

Florida has two baseball teams competing in MLB; the Miami Marlins and the Tampa Bay Rays.

American Football

'Football' as it is known in the States is arguably the most popular of all American sports. The season for the professional league (the NFL) starts in August through February and games are televised several days a week during these months. A team of 11 players attempt to score points against the opposing team by advancing a brown oval ball up a 100 yard field and into the opposing team's 'End Zone'. The ball can either be run with or thrown to another teammate in order to achieve this. The team advances up the field through a series of 'plays' which is led and orchestrated by the team's Quarterback.

Istockphoto: fredrocko

The National Football League (NFL) is made up of 32 teams and consists of 16 regular games followed by a series of play offs. The grand finale of the season is the 'Super Bowl', the Annual Championship game between the two Playoff winners. 'Super Bowl' is the biggest annual sporting event held in the United States and almost half of the U.S population tune in to watch the game.

Aside from the NFL, football fans can also get their fix by watching University games. College football teams compete against each other each season in the National Collegiate Athletic Association (NCAA). College cheerleaders and marching bands are also present to show their support and add to the atmosphere. College football can be just as popular to watch and follow by Americans as their professional counterparts and are typically televised Saturdays during the season.

The State of Florida has three football teams in the NFL: The Jacksonville Jaguars, the Miami Dolphins and the Tampa Bay Buccaneers. The most popular College football teams in Florida are: Tallahassee's Florida State University (the 'Seminoles'), Orlando's University of Central Florida (the 'Knights'), Gainesville's University of Florida (the 'Gators') and the University of Miami (the 'Hurricanes').

Basketball

Now to a Brit, basketball is the activity we used to do at school during a P.E lesson on a rainy day. America however, takes this sport to a whole new level. They did after all invent the game back in 1891 courtesy of a

Canadian born PE teacher called James Naismith living in Springfield, Massachusetts.

For those of us whose school days are distant memories, the objective of the game is to score points by shooting a basketball through a hoop positioned either end of the court. There are 5 players on a team and two points are scored for each basket made, unless the basket has been scored on or outside the 3 point line, in which case 3 points are scored. Players advance the ball down the court by bouncing it while moving or throwing it to a team mate.

The National Basketball Association (the NBA) is the nation's professional men's basketball league and it contains 30 teams (29 in the U.S and 1 in Canada). The season runs from October to June with each team playing 82 games before playoffs commence.

American Basketball has also received particular worldwide media attention thanks to the Olympic Games in recent years. In 1992, the so-called 'Dream Team' made up of the top American professional basketball players represented the United States in the Olympic Games for the first time. A few years later in 1996, the American Women's basketball team won the gold medal.

There are two Florida basketball teams in the NBA, the 'Miami Heat' and the 'Orlando Magic'.

Ice Hockey

'Hockey' as it's referred to in the States, isn't as popular as football, baseball and basketball but its popularity is growing. It's a very physical and fast game with a reputation for violence either from negligent hockey stick usage or punch ups between players. With 6 players on each team, (5 skaters and 1 goalie), skaters attempt to shoot the puck with their hockey sticks into their opponent's goal.

The major professional hockey league in North America is called the NHL (National Hockey League) and comprises of 23 U.S teams and 7 Canadian teams who compete for the Stanley Cup. Florida has two teams that play in the professional league, the Florida Panthers (based in Miami) and the Tampa Bay Lightning.

Motorsports

Formula 1 may be the preferred choice in Europe for race cars but in the States, stock car racing is more popular. NASCAR (National Association for Stock Car Auto Racing) is the largest stock car racing governing body. It's most famous races are; the Daytona 500, the Southern 500, the Coca-Cola 600 and the Brickyard 400.

The Daytona 500 happens to take place right here in Daytona Beach, Florida. It's a 500 mile stock car race held annually on the last Sunday of every February. It is sometimes referred to as 'the Great American Race' or the 'Superbowl' of Stockcar racing.

For those who prefer Formula 1 type racing, the Indianapolis 500 may be more up your alley. It's held in Speedway, Indiana on Memorial weekend (the last weekend in May). Also a 500 mile race, it has a seating capacity of over 250,000 and is labeled the 'The Greatest Spectacle in Racing'.

Soccer

For the avid British football fan I have some bad news for you. Football (or soccer as it is known in the States) is not a particularly popular sport. America does have a men's professional premier soccer league called the MLS (Major League Soccer) but it is not as followed or televised as the other popular sports discussed above. The MLS tends to lose its quality players to European teams, and as such, most soccer fans prefer to tune into English Premier League or European games rather than MLS ones given the choice. Some were hopeful that the signing of David Beckham at L.A Galaxy might ignite some interest in the sport across America but it did not materialize.

As of 2012, Major League Soccer consists of 19 clubs (16 from the U.S and 3 from Canada) and the season runs from March through October, with Playoffs and a Championship game in November.

Women's soccer favours a little better in America, thanks largely to their international success over recent years. In 1991, the U.S Women's national team won the first Women's World Cup and in 1996, the team won the first gold medal when the sport made its first appearance in the Olympic Games. Despite this, two attempts at establishing a women's professional league has not been successful. A third attempt is about to be launched where success appears more hopeful.

Happily, soccer is still popular among the youth in America and is one of the most played sports by kids in the U.S. That is until kids reach their teenage years. Many showing exceptional athletic ability are often encouraged to take up a more 'American' sport such as baseball, basketball or American football where they have the potential of earning millions in those professional leagues rather than a mediocre $30,000 in comparison playing in the professional U.S soccer league.

Youth soccer on a recreational basis is widely available through organizations such as the YMCA and local City leagues. Coaches however, typically consist of volunteer parents with limited knowledge of the game so standards tend to be below par.

There are still however opportunities for the more serious soccer players. Elite soccer programs exist which are designed to identify, nurture and maximize potential soccer talent. US Soccer Federation runs the Development Academy for boys and US Club Soccer, an Independent organization, runs the Elite Clubs National League for girls. Entry to these leagues are extremely competitive and players must show huge commitment and participate in frequent practices and tournaments that can be nationwide. Potential rewards though come in the form of college scholarships.

THE MLB TEAMS (BASEBALL)

DIVISION	AMERICAN LEAGUE TEAMS
East	Miami Marlins
East	Atlanta Braves
East	Washington Nationals
East	New York Mets
East	Philadelphia Phillies
West	Los Angeles Dodgers
West	San Diego Padres
West	San Fransisco Giants
West	Colorado Rockies
West	Arizona Diamondbacks
Central	Pittsburgh Pirates
Central	Chicago Cubs
Central	St Louis Cardinals
Central	Milwaukee Brewers
Central	Cincinnati Reds

DIVISION	NATIONAL LEAGUE TEAMS
East	Boston Red Sox
East	New York Yankees
East	Baltimore Orioles
East	Tampa Bay Rays
East	Toronto Blue Jays
West	L.A Angels of Anaheim
West	Oakland Athletics
West	Seattle Mariners
West	Texas Rangers
West	Houston Astros
Central	Chicago White Sox
Central	Minnesota Twins
Central	Detroit Tigers
Central	Cleveland Indians
Central	Kansas City Royals

THE NBA TEAMS (BASKETBALL)

DIVISION	EASTERN TEAMS
Atlantic	New York Knicks
Atlantic	Toronto Raptors
Atlantic	Philadelphia 76ers
Atlantic	Brooklyn Nets
Atlantic	Boston Celtics
Central	Chicago Bulls
Central	Detroit Pistons
Central	Indiana Pacers
Central	Milwaukee Bucks
Central	Cleveland Cavaliers
South East	Atlanta Hawks
South East	Miami Heat
South East	Orlando Magic
South East	Washington Wizards
South East	Charlotte Bobcats

DIVISION	WESTERN TEAMS
Northwest	Denver Nuggets
Northwest	Utah Jazz
Northwest	Portland Trail Blazers
Northwest	Oklahoma City Thunder
Northwest	Minnesota Timberwolves
Pacific	Los Angeles Clippers
Pacific	Los Angeles Lakers
Pacific	Phoenix Suns
Pacific	Sacramento Kings
Pacific	Golden State Warriors
Southwest	Dallas Mavericks
Southwest	New Orleans Hornets
Southwest	San Antonio Spurs
Southwest	Memphis Grizzlies
Southwest	Houston Rockets

THE NFL TEAMS (FOOTBALL)

DIVISION	AMERICAN CONFERENCE TEAMS
East	New York Jets
East	New England Patriots
East	Buffalo Bills
East	Miami Dolphins
West	San Diego Chargers
West	Denver Broncos
West	Kansas City Chiefs
West	Oakland Raiders
North	Pittsburgh Steelers
North	Cincinnati Bengals
North	Baltimore Ravens
North	Cleveland Browns
South	Jacksonville Jaguars
South	Tennessee Titans
South	Houston Texans
South	Indianapolis Colts

DIVISION	NATIONAL CONFERENCE TEAMS
East	Dallas Cowboys
East	Washington Redskins
East	Philadelphia Eagles
East	New York Giants
West	Seattle Seahawks
West	Arizona Cardinals
West	St Louis Rams
West	San Francisco 49rs
North	Green Bay Packers
North	Chicago Bears
North	Minnesota Vikings
North	Detroit Lions
South	New Orleans Saints
South	Atlanta Falcons
South	Tampa Bay Bucs
South	Carolina Panthers

Chapter 13

Immigration Methods

Immigrating to the United States is actually a lot harder to do than many people realize. Without family already living in the Country or at least half a million dollars in a bank account, the immigration path for a Brit is not usually an easy ride and can cause many to give up on their American dream.

Immigration systems in some countries such as Canada or Australia work on a point system. In these countries, the hopeful immigrant needs to reach a certain number of points in order to be granted permanent residency in that country. Points are typically awarded on the individual's level of education, employment experience, whether they can speak the native language or if they have family already living in the country.

America's immigration system however, does not work on such a point system. Typically, the British can only gain permanent residency through one of three ways: family, employment or through investment. As we look at each of these options in turn, it is important to remember that the following is intended only as an overview. It is not in any way legal advice and readers must discuss with an immigration lawyer the best options available to them.

British individuals living in the States are likely to be doing so under either a visa, green card or through citizenship. Each status holds different rights, conditions and privileges.

Green Card Holders

The official name for a green card holder is 'Lawful Permanent Resident (LPR) and it allows a person to live and work in the United States on a permanent basis. Green card status is valid for life but the card itself must be renewed every 10 years.

Green card holders have many more benefits and privileges than those living in the U.S on visas. Benefits include:

- Permission to work for any company without restrictions or the need for employer sponsorship. (The exception to this are companies who only hire U.S citizens usually for security reasons).

- The ability to re-enter the United States without the risk of being denied entry by Immigration at the Port of Entry.

- Eligibility for Social Security benefits upon retirement, providing the holder has worked for 10 years in the States before retiring.

- The ability to sponsor your spouse and all unmarried children under 21 for green cards themselves.

- Many companies require their clients to be lawful permanent residents or U.S citizens before offering their services. It can therefore be easier

- to obtain such things as mortgages, life and health insurance as a green card holder.

- A Green Card holder is eligible to apply for U.S Citizenship after 3-5 years depending on their circumstances. Citizenship brings further benefits.

To retain a green card, holders must ensure that they don't violate certain criminal or immigration laws which can be quite strict. One law for example, requires the holder to notify immigration authorities within 10 days of changing address.

As well as risking revocation of the card by committing a criminal offence, leaving the U.S for certain time periods can also jeopardize your LPR status. You may be considered abandoning your permanent resident status if you remain outside of the U.S for more than one year without obtaining a re-entry permit or returning resident visa. Additionally, any length of absence might be considered as abandonment if they believe you are moving to another country in order to live there permanently.

Citizenship

You can apply to become a U.S citizen after five years of owning a green card (3 years if the green card was obtained through marriage). Citizenship comes with a number of benefits. For example:

1. As a US citizen, you can sponsor your parents, spouse and qualifying children with minimal wait time. You can

also sponsor older children and brothers and sisters although there is a long waiting period for this.

2. You can vote in Federal elections.

3. You are not restricted to the amount of time you spend outside of the United States.

4. More jobs are open to you as most government positions require U.S citizenship.

5. You cannot be deported if you commit any illegal activity.

6. Some financial aid grants and college scholarships are only open to U.S citizens.

Obtaining a Green Card

Getting your hands on permanent resident status in the U.S is often no easy task. Ways to obtain a green card for a Brit often fall into one of the following three categories:

Family Based Residency

You may be eligible for a green card if you:

- Are an immediate relative of a U.S Citizen, (such as a spouse, unmarried child under 21 or parent).

- A family member of a U.S Citizen (such as unmarried children over 21, married children of any age and brothers and sisters).

132

- A family member of a green card holder. (i.e., their spouse or unmarried child).

- A member of a special category (such as a battered spouse of widower of a U.S citizen).

Many of the categories have limits on the number of people who can immigrate each year. This means that in the majority of cases there is usually a waiting period, which can sometimes be quite substantial. Generally, the more 'immediate' the family member is, the quicker the process, but as an example, the waiting time for a U.S citizen petitioning their brother or sister is currently over ten years.

Through Employment

Gaining residency through employment is actually more difficult than might first appear. In many cases, employers are first required to obtain certification from the U.S Department of Labor to show that 1. there aren't enough U.S workers who are willing, qualified and available, and 2, that no American workers will be displaced by foreign workers. In order to show this, employers go through a process called PERM (Program Electronic Review Management) where they must perform a series of recruitment tasks to test the job market.

As well as Labor Certification, a permanent and full time job offer is required and your employer must be able to prove the ability to pay the offered wage. Again, there are limits on the amount of people that can immigrate under this category each year so a long backlog exists.

For the talented Brits among us, you may be eligible for a green card through a first preference EB-1 or second preference EB-2 visa.

The EB-1 Visa:

If you have an extraordinary ability, are an outstanding professor or researcher or a multi-national executive or manager you may fit into this category.

Extraordinary Ability:

'Extraordinary ability' means a level of expertise indicating that the individual is one of that small percentage who has risen to the top of his or her field of endeavor. The alien must have sustained national or international acclaim in the field of science, art, education, business or athletics, which must be recognized in the form of extensive documentation. No offer of employment is required and no labor certification but the person must be seeking to enter the U.S to continue work in that field.

Outstanding professors and researchers

An alien may qualify under this category if they are recognized internationally as outstanding in a specific academic area, has at least 3 years of experience in teaching or research in the academic area and has the required offer of employment.

Multinational Executives & Managers

To be eligible under this category the alien must have been employed outside of the U.S in the three years preceding the petition and for at least 1 year by a firm or corporation in a managerial or executive capacity. The individual must be seeking to enter the United States in order to continue employment with the same employer or subsidiary or affiliate of them, and the petitioning employer must be U.S and have been in business for at least 1 year.

The EB-2 Visa:

Persons with advanced degrees or exceptional ability.

Exceptional ability is considered 'a degree of expertise significantly above that ordinarily encountered in the sciences, arts or business'. In proving such ability, you must show at least three of USCIS's ten criteria and must generally be accompanied by an approved job offer and labor certification.

An advanced degree professional is a member of the professions holding an advanced degree or equivalent or baccalaureate degree plus at least five years of progressive experience in the specialty. The offer of employment must require an advanced degree.

Investment: The EB-5 Visa:

For the wealthy Brits out there, green cards can often be obtained by making a substantial investment.   To be eligible you must invest in a commercial enterprise in the U.S of at least 1 million dollars or $500,000 if the investment is being made in a targeted employment area. It must be shown that the investment will benefit the U.S economy and create full-time employment for at least 10 qualified United States workers.   In return, the investor is rewarded with a conditional permanent residency which also extends to their spouse and any unmarried children under 21 years of age.

Non Immigrant Visas

There are a variety of non-immigrant visas available which give people the opportunity to live in the U.S on a temporary basis. Some of the more common ones used by Brits are listed below:

B2 Visa

A B-2 visa is a tourist visa which is typically six months in length.   It allows the holder to travel to the U.S for vacation or for medical treatment. Employment is not allowed.

L-1 Visa Intracompany Transferees

The L-1 visa is used to transfer employees from a company abroad to work in their company, subsidiary or affiliate in the U.S for a temporary period. The employee must have been working as a manager or executive or in a position that requires specialist knowledge for at least 1 year in the previous 3 years with that company abroad. The position in the U.S must also be one of managerial, executive or one that requires specialist knowledge.

The spouse of the employee and any unmarried children under 21 years of age may also accompany them. This type of visa is often a popular alternative to the E-2 visa as it has the ability to provide a route to green card status.

K Visas

K-1 visa allows the fiancé or fiancée of a U.S Citizen to travel to the U.S for the purpose of marrying that citizen within 90 days after entry. The process must be initiated by the U.S citizen. After marriage, the spouse would then be eligible for permanent residency based on being an immediate relative of a U.S Citizen. Under this visa, any unmarried children of the fiancé can accompany them under a K-2 visa providing they are under 21 years of age. K-3 and K-4 visas allow a spouse of a U.S citizen and the spouse's eligible children to travel and live in the U.S while waiting for permanent residency.

H-1B Visa.

This visa is for workers in specialty occupations. These are defined as occupations which require a US baccalaureate degree or equivalent in a field related to the occupation. Examples are lawyers, engineers and architects. If the applicant does not hold such a degree then they need the equivalent in a combination of education and work experience instead. Labor certification is also required.

E-2 Visa Treaty Traders & Investors

Over recent years, E-2 visas have become a common method for Brits to live in America. Rising house prices during the last two decades and a strong pound against the dollar meant that many British could afford to sell their home or other assets and have enough capital to invest in the U.S.

By purchasing a qualifying existing business or start up business, the visa allows the investor, together with his immediate family to live in the U.S in order to 'direct and develop the operations of the enterprise'.

For a successful application it must meet strict criteria, which is why it's vital to consult with an immigration lawyer to check you qualify before making such an investment. Part of the criteria is that the applicant must have invested or be actively in the process of investing, own at least 50% of the business, and that the investment must be 'substantial'. The business needs to be able to employ U.S workers and generate enough income to support the investor and their family.

E-2 visas issued in London are typically granted for a two year period. Thereafter, if the investor shows that the business has been performing well and still meets the criteria, the visa is often renewed for periods of five years. The investor's spouse and unmarried children under 21 may accompany the visa holder as E-2 dependants and spouses may also apply for work authorization.

It is important to remember that the E-2 visa is a non-immigrant visa, which means that the investor can only live in the U.S on a temporary basis. When the investor no longer develops and directs the operations of the enterprise they become ineligible. There must always be an intention to depart the United States when the visa ends.

The Drawbacks of Living on an E-2 Visa

E-2 visas can often provide Brits with the opportunity to live and experience a new life in America. However it does come with a number of downsides:

The Expense:

As well as the 'substantial' investment already made to secure the E-2 visa, living on one often means regular further expense. Being on a 'temporary' status means that many things are provided to you for only a short amount of time before they need renewal such as driver licenses and work authorization cards.

And when it comes to renewing the visa in year 2, you will need more funds. The renewal is required to be done in person by interview at the U.S Embassy of your native land. Therefore you will need cash for transatlantic flights, accommodation, visa fees and for the services of an immigration lawyer to compile your renewal application.

Finally for an E-2 holder, your stay in the United States is ultimately dependant on the success of your business and in a tough U.S economy it can be difficult to maintain a thriving enterprise. You are therefore prone to throwing every bit of your time and money into the business in order to keep it successful and many Brits on this visa work much longer hours than they did back in the U.K.

The Uncertainty:

Having obtained the E2 visa, you are well aware that your stay in the U.S is only temporary. You may be planning on staying for 2 years or 20. Who knows how successful your business will be and when you will yearn to return home to Britain. It is inevitable though that the longer you stay in the U.S, the more settled you will become. A house will become a home. Your children will settle in at school and will make friends. You and your spouse will make friends through work, expat connections and social activities.

Whatever your plans, the length of your stay will ultimately be in the hands of both the U.S Embassy renewing the visa and the immigration officials at the port of entry (who still have the authority to refuse entry into the country even with possession of a visa). There will be times when you and your family are standing in front of these officials not knowing which direction your lives are about to take.

The Dangers of Children 'timing out':

There aren't many investors that would be interested in moving to the U.S if their spouse and children weren't able to come with them. USCIS addresses this by allowing the spouse and any unmarried children under 21 to accompany the investor. However the situation changes dramatically when those children reach 21 years of age.

Once the investor's children reach 21, they are no longer classed as 'dependants' and are no longer eligible to remain in the States under their current status. In order to stay, these young adults would have to find their own visa such as a student visa, employment visa or instead through marriage.

As an example, investors with an 18 year old child will find that their son or daughter can only remain in the country for a maximum of three years under the E-2 program even though their parents may be able to remain for much longer. In contrast, younger children may have much more time but can find themselves having to return to the U.K at 21, to a country they know very little about after being brought up in America. It's an issue that E-2 holders must be aware of and take into serious consideration.

Chapter 14

National Holidays
And Other Celebrations

Wondering one day why all the kids are going to school dressed in green? Why the bank turns out to be closed courtesy of Christopher Columbus? Why you're being crushed in Walmart the day after Thanksgiving when you only popped in for a loaf of bread?

The U.S has many public holidays and celebrations throughout the year and many of them will be unfamiliar to us Brits. This chapter provides details of some of the major ones, including their dates, how they are usually celebrated and the American history behind some of them.

New Year's Day

New Year's Day on January 1st is a National Holiday in the United States and most businesses are closed. As in the U.K, the day is typically spent recovering from parties from the night before and making ambitious resolutions to lose weight, stop smoking and exercise more.

Martin Luther King Day

Martin Luther King was an important civil rights activist. He campaigned to end racial segregation on public transport and for racial equality in the United States. He was the youngest man to be awarded the Nobel Peace Prize and is well remembered for his 'I have a dream' speech. Following his assassination in 1968, a campaign was started for his birthday to become a holiday to honour him.

Martin Luther King Day is now a Federal Holiday and is held on the 3rd Monday of every January. Many

145

Government Departments and businesses are closed. Schools and colleges either close or stay open and teach their students about his life and work. It's typically regarded as a day to promote equal rights for all Americans.

Groundhog Day

I swear I'm not making this one up. February 2nd in the United States is 'Groundhog Day'. Tradition has it that on this day, if the Groundhog comes out of its burrow and sees its shadow, then it will be frightened by it and return to its hole. This indicates that there will be six more weeks of winter. If however, the groundhog comes out of his hole and does not see its shadow, it means that spring is on the way.

Although some States have adopted their own groundhogs, the official groundhog lives near Punxsutawney in Pennsylvania. The town attracts many visitors and media reporters each year on Feb 2nd to await the groundhog's appearance and his weather prediction.

Presidents Day / Washington's Birthday

'Washington's Birthday' is a Federal Holiday in the United States and held on the 3rd Monday of every February. It is also known as President's Day. The Holiday honours the life and work of George Washington, the first President of the United States but commemorates past presidents as well. Many businesses open as usual.

St Patrick' Day

St Patrick's Day is on March 17th and unlike the U.K, it's widely celebrated in the United States. Large street parades are held in many of the major U.S cities and Irish themed parties are in abundance across America. The colour green is exhibited and sometimes very creatively. People celebrating will not only dress in green clothing but also often consume food and drink that has been dyed green. Even the water in public places is sometimes changed, like the Chicago River dyed green for St Patricks' Day in 2005. The day is a celebration of Irish-American culture in the U.S, but it also provides a great way for Americans to act silly, go drinking and let their hair down at least once a year.

Easter

Unlike the U.K, Good Friday and Easter Monday are not official holidays in the United States and are working days. Churches will hold special services and Easter eggs are still a tradition. Easter Egg hunts are common activities for children to partake in over the Easter Weekend and there is even an egg rolling race on the lawn of the White House on Easter Monday. It is traditional to eat ham on Easter Sunday.

Cinco de Mayo

Cinco de Mayo is Spanish for 5th of May. It is a festival of Mexican pride and heritage on the anniversary of Mexico's victory for independence from French forces. It's not a federal holiday and businesses and schools are open as usual.

Memorial Day

Memorial Day is a federal holiday and is observed on the last Monday of May. It commemorates all men and women who have died in military service for the United States. Many Government offices are closed as are businesses and schools. It's traditional to fly the flag of the United States at half-mast from dawn until noon and many people visit cemeteries and memorials. Aside from remembrance, many people also take the opportunity to use the three day weekend to go on short breaks or hold family gatherings.

Independence Day

In 1775, America's 13 colonies were under the rule of England. The American people were tired of the taxes that England imposed on them and unrest began to grow. British troops were sent to quash any signs of rebellion but despite repeated attempts by the colonists, the crisis could not be resolved peacefully.

In 1776, the Colonies' 2nd Congress meeting in Philadelphia formed a committee with the express purpose of drafting a document which would formally sever their ties with England. The committee included Thomas Jefferson, Benjamin Franklin and John Adams. The resulting 'Declaration of Independence' was published on July 4th 1776.

The Declaration was then read to cheering crowds and the ringing of bells. The War of Independence continued for several years until 1783 and the 4th July became an official holiday.

Independence Day is highly celebrated and many Americans are off from work. It's a day of family celebrations with bbqs, public events and fireworks. Many people display the American flag on their homes.

Labor Day

Labor Day is held on the first Monday of every September. It's a Federal holiday and Government offices, schools and most businesses are closed. It originates from the Central Labor Union wishing to create a holiday for workers. It's an opportunity for Americans to have a 3 day weekend in the last days of the summer months.

Patriot Day

Patriot Day is on September 11th each year and is an observance to remember those who died and were injured in the terrorist attacks on the Twin Towers in New York, the Pentagon in Washington and the downed aircraft in Pennsylvania on 11th September 2001. It's not a Federal holiday and businesses and schools do not close, but many observe a moment of silence and fly the

American flag at half-mast as a sign of respect and remembrance.

Columbus Day

Columbus Day is on the second Monday of every October. It's to celebrate the anniversary of Christopher Columbus discovering America in 1492 but the public holiday is quite controversial. When Columbus discovered the country, America was already inhabited by the indigenous peoples and the European settlement that followed after its discovery, led to the deaths of a large portion of these native people. It has also been argued that as Columbus only discovered the Caribbean Islands and not mainland America itself, he shouldn't be honoured with the discovery at all.

Columbus Day is a Public Holiday in Florida and in many other U.S States but not in all States due to its' controversy. In Florida, non-essential Government offices and schools are closed but businesses usually stay open.

Halloween

Halloween is traditionally celebrated in Britain by children and teens dressing up in costumes and 'trick or treating' around the neighbourhood. Unfortunately, youth anti-social behavior has spoiled Halloween celebrations in Britain in recent years making it more of an unwelcome event than one to look forward to.

In Florida however, Halloween is celebrated in a much more family friendly way. Typically communities will embrace Halloween with many Americans decorating their front gardens with all things spooky. Children will trick and treat around the neighbourhood in the early evening and many adults hold Halloween costume parties in their homes. In Central Florida, a number of theme parks such as Universal Studios and Busch Gardens transform their grounds on select October evenings into Halloween events complete with haunted houses and scary characters roaming the parks.

Thanksgiving

Thanksgiving is a national holiday held on the 4th Thursday of every November. It's a day for families and friends to get together for a special meal and give thanks for what they have. It has a very similar feel to that of Christmas Day. Even a traditional roast turkey meal with potatoes, vegetables, gravy and cranberry sauce is typically served.

The history of Thanksgiving is as follows: In 1620, a ship called 'The Mayflower' left Plymouth, England with 102 passengers on board seeking a new life in the New World. Eventually landing in Massachusetts, only half of them made it through a brutal winter of exposure and disease. In the Spring of 1621, the Pilgrims were greeted by two Native Americans who taught them how to live off the land and to form an alliance with the Wampanoag, a local native tribe.

In November 1621, after the Pilgrims' first corn harvest proved successful, a celebratory feast was organized and shared with the Wampanoag Indians. Pilgrims then held their second Thanksgiving celebration in 1623 to mark the end of a long draught that had threatened the year's harvest. From then on, days of thanksgivings were celebrated by individual colonies and states until in 1863, President Abraham Lincoln proclaimed a national Thanksgiving Day to be held each November.

Black Friday

Black Friday is the day after Thanksgiving. It's a busy shopping day where stores will have sale events. It's very similar to the Boxing Day sales in the U.K. The advantage of the U.S version however, is that this shopping day is *prior* to Christmas unlike Boxing Day. It's therefore a great opportunity to purchase presents for Christmas at reduced prices.

Black Friday is not a Federal holiday, although it is a holiday in some states. Many people take the day off work so that the can have an extended Thanksgiving weekend.

Christmas Day

Christmas Day is celebrated in America just as in Britain. A day for families to come together, share gifts and for children to wait eagerly for the arrival of Santa Claus. In Florida, the warm weather on Christmas Day may take a little getting used to, but all the festivities and hype of Christmas still remain. Bear in mind that there is no Boxing Day holiday in the U.S, so if you typically need the 26th December to recover from your over indulgence, you will need to request an annual leave day from work.

Chapter 15

Verbal Confusion:

British & American Terminology

We may speak the same language but not all words are universally recognized. Substitute these British words into their American equivalents to greatly reduce blank American stares.

FOOD & DRINK

BRITISH	AMERICAN
Aubergine	Eggplant
Biscuit	Cookie
Candy Floss	Cotton Candy
Chips	(French) Fries
Courgette	Zucchini
Crisps	(Potato) Chips
Icing	Frosting
Ice Lolly	Popsicle
Jam	Jello
Jelly	Jello
Jacket Potato	Baked Potato
Sweets	Candy

DRIVING

BRITISH	AMERICAN
Bonnet	Hood
Boot	Trunk
Caravan	Trailer
Car Park	Parking Lot
Central Reservation	Median
Diversion	Detour
Estate Car	Station Wagon
Fly-Over	Overpass
Exhaust Pipe	Tail Pipe
Gear Lever	Stick Shift
Junction	Intersection
Kerb	Curb
Lay-By	Rest Stop
Lorry	Truck
Motorway	Highway
Number Plate	Licence Plate
Pavement	Sidewalk
Petrol	Gas
Roundabout	Traffic Circle
Zebra Crossing	Pedestrian Crossing

CLOTHES

BRITISH	AMERICAN
Dungarees	Overalls
Jumper	Sweater
Pants	Underwear
Swimming Costume	Swimsuit
Trainers	Sneakers
Tights	Pantyhose
Trousers	Pants
Vest	Undershirt
Waistcoat	Vest
Wellington Boots	Galoshes

SCHOOL

BRITISH	AMERICAN
Full Stop	Period
Headmaster/Mistress	Principal
Lollipop Man/Lady	Crossing Guard
Math	Maths
Open Evening	Open House
Playtime	Recess
Rubber	Eraser
Rucksack	Backpack

OBJECTS

BRITISH	AMERICAN
Hoover	Vacuum Cleaner
Lift	Elevator
Mobile Phone	Cell Phone
Plaster	Band Aid
Sellotape	Sticky Tape
Torch	Flashlight

LEISURE

BRITISH	AMERICAN
Holiday	Vacation
Bank Holiday	National Holiday
Film	Movie
Cinema	Movie Theater
Advert (TV)	Commercial
Football	Soccer
Pitch (sports)	Field
Ring (telephone)	Call
Mate	Friend
Naughts & Crosses	Tic Tac Toe
Draughts	Checkers
Skipping Rope	Jump Rope

HOME RELATED

BRITISH	AMERICAN
Flat	Apartment
Semi-Detached	Duplex
Terraced	Townhouse
Ground Floor	1st Floor
1st Floor	2nd Floor
Garden	Yard
Housing Estate	Sub Division
Lavatory	Restroom
Skirting Boards	Baseboards
Tap	Faucet
Rubbish	Trash/Garbage
Cooker	Stove
Grill	Broil
Curtains	Drapes
Duvet	Comforter
Flannel	Wash Cloth
Kitchen Roll	Paper Towel
Washing Up Liquid	Dish Soap
Wardrobe	Closet

CHILD RELATED

BRITISH	AMERICAN
Cot	Crib
Dummy	Pacifier
Nappies	Diapers
Pram	Baby Carriage
Pushchair	Stroller

PLACES

BRITISH	AMERICAN
Accident & Emergency	Emergency Room (ER)
Chemist	Pharmacy
Housing Estate	Sub-Division
Off Licence	Liquor Store
Pub	Bar
Shop/Supermarket	Grocery Store

MISCELLANEOUS

BRITISH	AMERICAN
Autumn	Fall
Bill	Check
City Centre	Downtown
CV	Resume
Estate Agent	Realtor
Fortnight	2 Weeks
Fringe (Hair)	Bang
Naught	Zero
Parcel	Package
Post	Mail
Postage & Packaging	Shipping & Handling
Queue	Line
Sacked	Fired
Trolley	(Shopping) Cart
Skip	Dumpster
Surname	Last Name

Useful Links

Fl Department of Highway Safety & Motor Vehicles.
www.flhsmv.gov

Internal Revenue Service
www.IRS.gov

United States Citizenship & Immigration Services.
www.USCIS.gov

The U.S Social Security Administration.
www.socialsecurity.gov

Fl Department of State Division of Corporations.
www.sunbiz.org

Florida Department of Revenue
www.dor.myflorida.com

Florida Department of Education.
www.fldoe.org

Florida Department of Health.
www.doh.state.fl.us

Florida Weather Center.
www.flaweather.com

National Hurricane Center
www.nhc.noaa.gov

Federal Emergency Management Agency
www.fema.gov

British Embassy for the United States website.
www.ukinusa.fco.gov.uk

Expat Forums:

www.britsinamericanetwork.us

www.britishexpats.com

www.britishabroad.com

www.expatforum.com

INDEX

About the Author

Lisa Crane grew up in Norfolk, England, graduating from the University of East Anglia with a degree in law. After military service in the Royal Air Force as a commissioned officer, she spent 9 years as a police officer on the streets of Essex dealing with crime in society from anti-social behavior and public disorder to the investigation of serious and violent offences.

Following the birth of her two children, and after becoming increasingly disillusioned by what Britain had to offer, she moved to Florida for a 6 month trial period. Six years later, with no intention of returning to England, she lives happily in Orlando with her husband and her two very Americanized children.

13358983R00098

Printed in Great Britain
by Amazon